CHRIS McIVOR

Chris McIvor OBE has worked for the last 28 years in emergency response and development in countries as diverse as Sudan, Morocco, Algeria, Cuba, Haiti, Jamaica and Zimbabwe. He is currently Advocacy and Programme Development Director for the charity *Save the Children* in Mozambique.

He has published many articles about development issues in poorer countries, and was a frequent correspondent for the Irish Times between 1983 and 1986 and was Zimbabwe correspondent for New Africa and Africa Now magazines between 1986 and 1993. He is the author of several books on the environment, land reform in Zimbabwe, disabled peoples' rights, unaccompanied child migration as well as the principles and practice of community involvement in development programmes.

Chris McIvor has published short stories in a variety of journals across the world. Much of his writing reflects his experience in Africa as well as his home background in the far north of Scotland, where his parents still live. In 2005 he was awarded an OBE for his services on behalf of *Save the Children* in Zimbabwe.

A Bend in the Nile

My Life in Nubia and Other Places

Chris McIvor

SANDSTONEPRESS
HIGHLAND | SCOTLAND

First published in Great Britain in 2008 by
Sandstone Press Ltd,
PO Box 5725,
One High Street,
Dingwall,
Ross-shire,
IV15 9WJ,
Scotland.

www.sandstonepress.com

Editor: Robert Davidson

DUMFRIES & GALLOWAY LIBRARIES	
048291	
Askews & Holts	
J-15	

ISBN-10: 1-905207-25-5
ISBN-13: 978-1-905207-25-1

Cover by River Design, Edinburgh.

Typeset in Linotype Sabon by Iolaire Typesetting, Newtonmore
Printed and bound by Bell & Bain, Glasgow

This book is dedicated to my father, Sandy McIvor, whose love of travel inspired my own curiosity about far off places.

Contents

Acknowledgements

This book was written from notes, articles I wrote for various newspapers and magazines, and abiding memories that have stayed with me from my time in Sudan. The Sudanese who welcomed me into their homes and communities are too numerous to mention, but Abdel Atif, Abdel Majid in Dongola and Mohammed Ad Din in El Geneina deserve a special mention for their guidance and wisdom.

Although the scheme that brought English teachers to Sudan in the 1980s had several flaws, it provided an opportunity for all of us who went there to grow and develop. That experience has inspired many of us ever since. I constantly bump into friends and colleagues in the aid world who started off their professional lives as teachers in Sudan, and who date their motivation to become involved in this line of work in honour of that experience.

This book owes a huge debt to Robert Davidson of Sandstone Press, whose interest in my work and my life in different parts of Africa pushed me to write it. I would also like to acknowledge Moira Forsyth for her editorial assistance, and my twin sister, Gisela, for her feedback on the text as it developed and her constant encouragement.

I would also like to acknowledge the Irish Times, New African, Africa Now, Africa Events, Development and Co-operation Magazine, Sudanow, and my local newspaper in Scotland, the Caithness Courier, for having published several articles I wrote during the time I spent in North Africa.

1

Leave your preconceptions behind

The flight from London via Rome to Khartoum had been scheduled to depart early morning for arrival late in the day.

'A technical problem has developed,' a mechanical voice explained several hours after we still hadn't left, prompting George, beside me, to comment that we would be lucky to get there before midnight.

'The airline is completely unreliable,' he sighed. 'But you'll get used to it.'

George had been a teacher in Sudan for the past year. Now returning for a second stretch he was an expert compared to the rest of us. At various times during that morning, we gathered in small clusters around him to ask how it had been, what we should expect. Would we get malaria? Did the schools have books and the houses running water?

Flattered by the attention George freely shared his opinions about the country. His predictions about the officials, the schools we would teach in and the people were similar to his characterization of the airline. As the picture grew more dismal I remembered the advice of my interviewer from the Sudanese Ministry of Education, cautioning me not to pay too much attention to what others would say about his country.

'Try to leave your preconceptions behind,' he said, after informing me I had the job and would be travelling to Khartoum the following week. 'Above all else, make up your own mind.'

We left London for Rome four hours behind schedule, and there our group of thirty shrank to twenty-six when some of our number disappeared, delaying our flight onwards for another three hours. Only when someone informed the authorities that the missing teachers had entered and exited the aircraft with their entire baggage did it become clear they were not late, delayed, kidnapped or ever likely to return. They had organized a scam to acquire a free flight to Italy and pocketed the advance money.

A few hours later the pilot announced we were approaching land. Libya was somewhere beneath us and, although it was dark, we could see out of the window a ribbon of lights that marked where the Mediterranean Sea washed against the coast of Africa. A few minutes later they were swallowed up by a blackness that remained unbroken for several hours. It was unlike the previous landscapes we had passed over where villages and towns announced themselves below us with their occasional illumination.

'Desert all the way to Khartoum,' said a voice beside me, and only then did I fully understand I had reached a point, in my mind as much as in physical space, from which it would be difficult to return. Unable to see ahead, my thoughts returned to the immediate past.

'Why do you want to work in Sudan?' Taleb, my interviewer, asked me.

We were sitting in the Sudanese Cultural Centre, a small annex to the embassy in London. The centre itself was little more than a room with some crafts on the wall beside pictures of faces that seemed just too happy. A caption underneath them read, 'Welcome to Sudan, the Warm Heart of Africa.

Taleb was very dark, looked uncomfortable in his suit and tie and seemed uninterested in my answers to his questions. He told me he had been interviewing prospective teachers for most of the day and was somewhat fatigued. If I had said to him I had nothing better to do with my life than explore his country I believe he would still have appointed me.

As it was I told him the half-truths we usually come out with on those occasions when we want a job, when we give the kind of answers we expect someone wants to hear. Yes, I had wanted to visit Sudan for a long time. I was fascinated by Africa and intrigued by its biggest country. Sure, I wanted to help people more unfortunate than myself. I did not tell him that a few months previously I had been beating my brains over a philosophy thesis in a college in Ireland.

'But who is it for?' my father had asked me one evening. 'Who on earth could be interested in such an obscure topic as the influence of Hegel on Karl Marx?' A practical, pragmatic man he would never understand why I didn't philosophize in my 'spare time' and regularly pointed out that I would never earn any money sitting in a room and pondering the nature of the universe.

'The only thing you'll learn is to be philosophical about not getting a job.

Lives aren't altered by such observations of course, unless our own thoughts have already veered in that direction. His remarks crystallized a lot of doubts I had at the time about my suitability for academia, about the relevance of my research to the world outside the walls of the college. When I saw an advert in a newspaper requesting graduates to come and work in Sudan, the prospect of travel appealed to me. I sent off my application hardly expecting a reply. In truth, I had only a vague idea where Sudan actually was. I could recall some images from a film with Charlton Heston and Laurence Olivier entitled 'General Gordon of Khartoum'. I had no prior experience to offer, no travels in Africa to indicate that I might be suitable. 'Why would they want you?' I asked myself. To my surprise a few days later I was invited for the interview in London.

Now, only a week later, I was on a plane above the Sahara. Looking around I wondered if the other teachers had nobler motives. Part of me was concerned that I had none of the missionary zeal that some of them displayed, although I wondered about that. I had no reason to doubt their sincerity, but I remembered too my interviewer's advice about not carrying too much baggage, that I should avoid carrying a set of expectations that might clash with the reality of the country.

As George had predicted we began our descent to Khartoum a few minutes after midnight. Looking down onto the city's

sparse lights I resolved to meet my new life with whatever
flexibility, receptivity and lack of preconception I could manage. I would travel as lightly as I could.

International airports usually inhabit their own self-enclosed
and protected spaces, separate from the noise and turmoil and
characteristics of their cities. Travellers move between them as
if stepping from one familiar room to the next. A comfortable
cocoon of plush shops, smart restaurants and privileged
treatment shuts out the world beyond the fences.

When George told us 'Don't expect much when we fly into
Khartoum,' we had imagined something only slightly different
from what we had been used to. His warning did not prepare
us for what we actually found. Khartoum airport was more
like a bus station or a busy market than anything we had
previously encountered. Not only had the city swept up to its
doorstep but obstinately and intrusively pushed its way inside.

As we stepped off the plane an official ushered us into a
building where immigration officials and customs officers
were hard to distinguish from a noisy crowd of taxi drivers,
vendors and excited family members awaiting the arrivals
from London. My first reaction was one of panic. Would I
find my luggage? Would I get separated from my colleagues?
Without a word of Arabic how would I understand the signs?
There was no one to meet us either, to help us negotiate our
way through a mass of people all of whom seemed to know
what they were doing.

Eventually the crowd thinned as families were collected and
taxi drivers and vendors disappeared with their customers. We
gathered together and agreed that the best thing to do was
camp and wait for morning when someone would surely fetch
us. It was uncomfortable in the heat and tempers began to
fray.

'I told you there would be no one here,' George gloated,
deriving some satisfaction from having his views confirmed, as
we shook our heads in irritation, preparing ourselves for his
other, even gloomier predictions. No one could sleep. Some
time in the early morning as I paced the floor, I bumped into

another traveller who had been waiting for a flight south for almost a week.

'You seem remarkably calm,' I observed.

'Why shouldn't I be? When there's nothing to do but wait there's no point in getting upset. Besides, the airport officials have made me welcome. They've arranged cushions for me to sleep on and food to eat whenever I get hungry.'

'But that's terrible!'

'It could be worse. A friend of mine was stranded in Juba for several months because of damage to the one aircraft that serviced the route.'

'Several months? Only one aircraft?' My heart sank with apprehension.

'Take it easy,' he counselled. 'You won't last long here if you get impatient.'

At daybreak George elected to go into the city to inform the relevant authorities that we had arrived. A few hours later he returned with a bus and a smiling official from the Ministry who apologized for what had happened.

'There was an announcement that you would not be arriving until this morning,' he told us. 'Inshallah, today will be better.'

That was the first time I heard the word that was to become so familiar, repeated on every occasion when a prediction or wish or intention about the future was made. I reached for my dictionary.

'Inshallah' meant 'God willing,' a sentiment that could never do justice to the depth of meaning and emotion the Sudanese give to the most frequently used word in their vocabulary. It was also the unofficial name of the airline we had flown since, as I was to discover, arrival and departure times were a mystery even to the people who ran it.

'I'll be back in a few days,' the Ministry official announced when we checked into our hotel. 'There will be forms to complete and then I'll be able to say where you will be posted. Until then, your time is your own.'

The palm trees that line the streets of Khartoum are one reminder of the desert that surrounds it. In summer too, during the heat of the day, clouds of sand and dust appear on the horizon driving people indoors until the storm has passed. Occasionally these clouds will carry rain and for a while at least the city acquires a freshness it lacks for most of the year. This temporary condition does not last and can never compete with the long, dry seasons that stretch on either side. It is the Nile that Khartoum has to thank for its existence, for without its water it would never have emerged from the parched landscape.

The markets are the centre from which the streets radiate outwards. The crowds of people that ebb and flow around them seem impossible to negotiate, as if they are controlled by some wilful spirit that pushed and pulls the individuals who compose it in a direction they are powerless to resist. As a stranger arriving for the first time, this mass of people, of jumbled traffic, has something terrifying about it. You worry that if you step into that river of moving humanity you might get lost, that it will encircle you and sweep you away.

The men on the streets are dressed in long, white gowns called jellabiyas. The women are brightly coloured with the scarves and shawls draped about them, which frame but do not cover their faces. Occasionally, the traffic will come to a stop and the temporary flow of people will be halted. From somewhere a line of camels has emerged to take centre stage, like a group of actors that the audience has been waiting for.

Despite the fact that they seem out of place in these cramped, narrow streets they glide forward oblivious of their environment, bringing with them for a while a hint of their desert home. The men on top of them ignore the blare of horns and shouts of irritation from the drivers who have to let them pass. They do not gesticulate or shout back, as if they have acquired something of the stateliness and indifference of the animals they ride. Although the life of the city instantly resumes when they disappear you feel that perhaps the streets and houses, the cars and crowds of people are the intruders here, that it is the world that the camels have brought with them that is the real heart of North Africa.

Venturing out at last, I suffered a few minutes panic before I learned, first, to push and shove against the crowd, then to relax and drift in whatever direction it happened to be moving. It was the market I wanted to visit and since that seemed to be where everyone else was heading, I muttered a quick 'Inshallah' and let myself go.

People stared: men, women and children. They had no qualms about displaying their interest in a stranger who had appeared among them. But there was no malevolence or hostility either. People shouted words I did not understand but the smiles behind them were sufficient to let me know I was not unwelcome, that their curiosity was not tinted by mistrust or fear.

That first day out, and in the days of exploration that followed, I was adopted, as were my colleagues who had embarked on their own excursions. Sooner or later someone would approach with broken English, an offer of help or assistance, a story about how they had met you before, introducing themselves as if they had known you for a long time.

John was tall, very tall, well over six feet, a characteristic he told me of the people he came from. He smiled a lot too, like one of the people in the photos I had seen back in London. When I told him several times that I did not need a guide, that I was fine on my own, his smile and friendly manner never altered.

'This is your first day in Khartoum, isn't it?' he asked. Was it so obvious? Did I look so out of place?

'Don't worry,' he said. 'I'll show you around,' and that was how we became friends.

He came from the south of Sudan. As he walked beside me, clearly having slowed his considerable pace to accommodate my own, he told me he was a refugee from the fighting that had been going on there for more years than he could remember. He had lost brothers and sisters in that war and now lived in a shantytown somewhere on the edge of the city. He was currently studying business English and he wanted to go to America.

Easy disclosures about personal history normally take much longer where I come from, but I was learning to travel with the current. He seemed disappointed when I told him I did not come from New York or Chicago.

'Where is Scotland?' he asked.

'In the United Kingdom.'

He shrugged his shoulders, indicating he had never heard of it. 'Name a city nearby.'

'London' I said and the penny dropped. Yes, he had heard of London. 'Scotland is north of London' is what we finally settled on, and it was enough for him to fix my country in the map of the world he carried in his head.

The pushing and pulling of the crowd, the hot and dusty afternoon, the lack of sleep at the airport had made me tired. I allowed myself to be steered towards a café at the edge of the market. John ordered tea for both of us. Watching the people going about their business he told me he could tell which ethnic group and part of the country they came from.

'That person is a Shilluk from further south. From Malakal, probably.'

'How can you tell?'

'You see those marks on his forehead, the ones that look like raised bumps. That's how.' To prove his point John shouted to the stranger, who, unfazed by his question, confirmed that he did indeed come from Malakal and belonged to the group that John had named. I wondered how someone from Scotland would respond if I shouted to them in public to confirm where they came from. Whatever the reaction it would not be the same as the one I had just witnessed.

'That family are Dinka, my part of the country. Have you heard of Juba?' I remembered the name of the place where people had been stranded when the one aircraft never arrived, a dot on the large map of Sudan not far from the border with Kenya.

Noticing how impressed I was at his knowledge of the country he added, 'It is our different groups that distinguish us. Here in Sudan we wear our ethnicity like a set of clothes.'

'Why?' I asked.

'To show who we are and who we belong to. Isn't that the same in your own country?'

I shook my head, thinking of the ubiquitous clothing of my generation, the jeans and jackets that never hinted of our respective nationalities let alone our 'ethnic' loyalties. All we had left was our accents, but something troubled me.

'Isn't that why there is conflict in Sudan today? Isn't ethnicity one of the reasons for your wars and fighting?'

I ventured the question, not knowing if I was intruding into a sensitive area. Was such a discussion appropriate a few minutes after meeting a stranger, and in a country where I was ignorant about everything?

John didn't seem to mind. He went on to tell me about the long history of conflict between the north and south of the country, about a more recent war that had broken out between two of the principal groups in southern Sudan vying for power when the first conflict had just finished.

Ethnicity, he said, was fine on its own but when it became corrupted by religion and politics it turned nasty and allowed people to be manipulated and exploited.

He also pointed out that one of the reasons north and south were fighting today was because of the politics of divide and rule the British had left behind. When Muslims fought against Christians, when one tribe attacked another, they had presented themselves as fair referees, the responsible adult who kept squabbling children apart, although many of these squabbles were provoked by the British themselves.

'This is happening today to serve the interests of our leaders. They play off one group against the other and when war breaks out they say they are the only people who can resolve it.'

'So don't you feel resentment towards them, the British that is? Don't you feel resentment towards me, a national of the country that once exploited you?'

John laughed. 'If I did I wouldn't be sitting here with you drinking tea.'

When John indicated that he would come to my hotel next day to show me the sights of the city I shrugged my shoulders. In truth I was suspicious as to what he might want. Why this attempt at friendship with a stranger who had only just arrived in his country? I also did not want any kind of commitment at this time, any limitations on my freedom to explore my new surroundings at my own pace and in my own way.

'You don't have to worry,' he said, as if reading my mind. 'I am not after your money. I will practise my English. That is all.'

Embarrassed that this was what I had indeed been thinking and at my tardy response to his offer of friendship I agreed. 'Where do you want to go?' he asked, when he turned up at the appointed time.

On a piece of paper the Ministry official had distributed, entitled 'Things to do while you wait in Khartoum', there was a note reminding us we had to register ourselves at the British consulate within a few days of our arrival. We might have to be flown home in an emergency, it ominously stated, or if we got 'in trouble' with the authorities a consular official would have to bail us out. John recognized the address I showed him. It was beside a museum we could visit and the Sudanese Club that was listed on my piece of paper.

A guard at the entrance refused to let John accompany me inside. 'Only people with British passports or a good reason to be here,' he insisted when we tried to get in. John shrugged his shoulders and told me he would wait.

Stepping into that building from the hot, dusty streets was like crossing a threshold between one reality and another. I was hit by a blast of cool air when I opened the door. There were English voices, signs in my own language, men in shirts and ties and women in floral dresses who looked no different from people you might find in an office in London on a warm day. Unlike in the markets there were orderly queues in different parts of the building. I found the one in front of the sign that read 'Visas and Registration.'

'How can I help you?' asked one of the women.

'I've come to register,' I replied. 'I'm new to Sudan.'

She asked for my passport and took down my details. 'Profession?' she asked.

'Teacher,' I answered, not expecting the subsequent look of irritation when I said so, as if I had indicated 'hooligan' or 'troublemaker' instead of something I had reason to be proud of.

'We've had issues with teachers in the past,' she said, her manner noticeably frostier. 'I hope you won't be a problem,' she added, handing me a form to sign where the word 'teacher' had been underlined as if it denoted a contagious disease.

'And if we have to fly you home,' she said, after I returned the signed form, 'we'll need your parents' address so as to get our money back.' The thought of my parents receiving a phone call asking them to bail out their son in Sudan filled me with horror. How could I claim at twenty-three to be standing on my own feet if I had to endure such a humiliation? I was determined not to be a problem, I told the lady behind the counter.

'Next!' she shouted, as if anxious to find someone with a more acceptable profession.

The Sudan Club was next on the list. I expected from the name that John would have no problem getting in, that there would be a flavour of the country I was to spend the next year in and an element of Sudanese culture I could quietly ease my way into. But an even surlier guard than the one at the consulate demanded a membership card, which I didn't have. He accepted the document accrediting me as a teacher, but insisted John would not be allowed inside

'No Sudanese,' he replied, even when I offered to pay the ridiculous amount of dollars that were needed to enter.

'Don't worry,' John said, as I was about to turn away. 'I have some business to look after. I'll come back in a few hours when you're finished.'

The Sudan Club should have been called the Empire Club or the Colonial Club or some other name that indicated its distance and separation from anything to do with the country. For five dollars a day you were allowed to enter a relic from a former era. High walls, barbed wire and security personnel delivered a clear message to the rest of Khartoum to keep out.

'Why is it on our list?' I wondered. Reading that piece of paper again I realized that a large number of the locations had "foreign" names, like the American Club, the British Council, the French Cultural Centre, the Roman Catholic Cathedral, the German Club, the Italian Club, as if whoever had compiled it imagined that as soon as we arrived in the country we would all be homesick.

I sat at a table beside a blue swimming pool, ill at ease and out of place. There were a few other people at the tables around me. A Sudanese waiter in a crisp, white uniform asked me what I wanted to eat. 'What do you have?' The special for the day was fish and chips, salad, and ice cream for dessert. Had I travelled several thousand miles to eat something I could find in any restaurant back home? There was no local dish on the menu. If I wanted something Sudanese I would have to go somewhere else.

'I'll have the chips,' I said, determined to get some benefit from the money I spent. John would be back in an hour. I could escape then.

An elderly gentleman sat at the table opposite drinking beer, something I thought was forbidden. 'Not in here,' he replied when I asked him. 'In the Sudan Club we can do what we like.'

Having lived and worked in the country for many years he had nothing good to say about it. He launched into a tirade about the bureaucracy, the corruption, the laziness of the Sudanese, the inefficiency of the transport system, the poor state of the hospitals and the electricity cuts that were becoming more frequent

'So what do you do?' he asked me, when he had finally exhausted his list of woes.

I paused for a while before answering 'teacher'. When I did so, I fancied I could see the same expression I had witnessed earlier, as if I had confessed something unsavoury and inappropriate. There had been an 'incident' a few months ago, he said. Some teachers had 'wandered in' and become argumentative, drunk and noisy.

'We're thinking of banning teachers,' he added, looking at

me as if I should make the most of being here since it would probably be my last visit.

I said to myself that there would be no need to ban me because I would never return. I ate my food as quickly as I could and walked out of the Sudan Club an hour after I had entered, five dollars poorer but considerably wiser.

John was outside and I wondered if he had really had any business to attend to or whether he was just being polite. 'Where to now?' he asked.

'Anywhere that is not on that stupid list,' I answered.

As it turned out, John was a poor guide and did not know much about the locations we visited. His usual answer to one of my queries was to shake his head. But I liked his honesty and willingness to admit he didn't know. He would translate my questions to strangers with considerable enthusiasm and a dogged persistence until they were answered.

I was less interested in visiting museums or 'famous sights', the usual buildings and places favoured by tourists. The sights and sounds of ordinary Khartoum were what I wanted to explore and for that I didn't need a professional guide but someone who lived there.

After a few days John felt comfortable enough to invite me to his own part of the city. This was a sprawling settlement on the edge of Khartoum largely comprised of southern refugees who had fled the previous war and the economic collapse brought with it. I found it difficult to conceal my shock at the poverty and squalor I saw when we got out of the taxi. The houses were cramped, squalid affairs seemingly constructed wherever space was available. Many of the children running around wore ragged clothes and had swollen bellies that reminded me of the images I had seen on television whenever an appeal was made to help 'the starving in Africa.'

When the wind came from the direction of the hill behind the shantytown it brought with it the pungent smell of rotting garbage from the dump where thousands of people deposited their rubbish. 'We are illegal here,' John said, 'and because of that the authorities don't help us.'

There was no electricity, running water or official services of any kind although the place had been in existence for years. 'The Government says if they made us official they would have to look after us. They say they don't have money but we wonder why they spend so much on the houses of the President or on the big hotel they are building in the centre of Khartoum.'

What most surprised me after getting over my first encounter with this level of poverty, was that the people around us seemed to be simply getting on with their lives. Whether along the narrow alleys we walked through or in the market, men and women could be seen laughing and joking with friends and neighbours, arguing over prices, shaking hands when a deal was struck. Children with ragged clothes and swollen stomachs played football in the middle of the street with a crude ball made out of paper and plastic bags, but the noises they made were no different from the shouting and laughter of children back home, of boys and girls having fun.

'I expected people to be more miserable,' I confided to John, thinking as I did how crass this must sound and how naive my assumption that I could begin to understand the lives of people so distant and removed from the circumstances of my own life.

John placed a hand on my shoulder. 'Poor people have their lives too. We make the best of them, just like you.'

Over the course of the week passers-by continued to stare, although less than before. The fact I was no longer on my own seemed to satisfy most. I felt less like a queer fish in a crowded pond and more at home until an event occurred that left me shaken, reminding me this was a country I still did not know.

We were in Omdurman, near the camel market that had become one of my favourite locations. From the café we heard a noise close by, the shouting of a large crowd of people. As it got nearer we could see a man running along the centre of the road. His clothes were torn, there was blood on his face, and people were pursuing him, shouting in excitement. Alerted by the noise others joined in. Suddenly the space in front of the man was cut off and there was nowhere left for him to run.

When the crowd closed in I could hear above their shouting

the noise of the blows as he was beaten. Two policemen beside us did not intervene. Only when the crowd retreated, leaving the body of the thief prostrate on the ground, did they move to investigate what was happening. I could not tell whether he was alive or dead, but the crowd had turned silent as if ashamed of what had been done, as if the punishment this time had gone too far.

John took my arm and led me away. 'You should not have seen this,' he said. 'You will get the wrong idea about our country.'

The Ministry official turned up the following week with a large map of Sudan. He called us together and spread it across a table.

'It is time to decide where you are going. Do any of you have a preference?'

More knowledgeable about the country, almost embarrassingly better prepared, my colleagues impressed me with names of provinces and towns I had never heard of. All of them seemed to know exactly where they wanted to go and what they wanted to do. At last the official came to me.

'I'm happy to go wherever I'm sent,' I said, and beside me the all-knowing George offered a wry smile.

'Good, we will send you to Dongola,' said the Ministry official, pointing to a small dot many miles from Khartoum. 'It is a wonderful place,' he added, raising some ironic laughter from the more experienced in the room. 'Have you heard? It is famed for its sturdy, white donkeys.'

I could see from the map that the interior was nothing but desert, and the only place names were beside the river. The rest of that vast area was coloured an empty yellow, with a few occasional palm trees to indicate an oasis. George told me later that to the east of Dongola was the Nubian Desert, to the west was the rest of the Sahara and for thousands of miles in either direction there was nothing but sand.

'Good luck,' he said, but what he really meant was 'You should have listened to what I told you.'

I accepted the decision stoically, more stoically than John

when I met him outside. 'Why are they sending you to the hottest part of our country?' he asked. 'It is miles away from anywhere. And there are no Christians either. Everyone in that province is Muslim'

'It's okay. I like the desert,' I replied, unable to think of a smarter answer, 'and it is near Egypt.' Truth to tell, these were the only things I knew about the place.

Next day, John took me to the bus terminal in the Suq Es-Shabi market, from where the northern buses departed. I had a ticket, some cash in advance of my salary, and a letter from the authorities to present on arrival. The map the Ministry official showed us had bright yellow lines stretching like the spokes of a wheel from Khartoum to all parts of the country. I was to find out, however, that these were mere tracks in the desert and not the tarmac and asphalt roads I had remembered on maps back home.

'What about this bus journey?' I asked apprehensively. 'I've been told it could take me a full day to get there.'

'You will be lucky to get there in two,' John replied, and ran off to buy me enough water for three.

The bus we eventually found was an old, rickety affair, with 'Jumbo Jet' written in bright yellow letters along the side. It looked as if it was held together by bits of wire and good luck, but the name made us laugh. When I presented the paper with the Ministry stamp that would take me 'anywhere in the country' the driver grew irritated. Having collected these papers for several years he had never seen a cent, but when John told him I was a teacher on my first assignment he pointed to a place beside him, which he said was the most comfortable on the bus.

'When will we leave?' I asked in the broken Arabic I had picked up from my guidebook and John and the few lessons the Ministry had provided in the course of the week.

'Inshallah today,' he said. 'It all depends on when we have enough passengers.'

Across the time span of a week there flew the memory of the traveller in the airport and the story about his stranded colleague. Was he still there, I wondered, sleeping on his cushions and eating when he was hungry.

Remember, I told myself, you won't last long here if you get impatient. The bus will leave when it is ready.

In a small shack beside the bus John and I drank tea and wrote our addresses down for each other. He also told me that the place he was staying was only temporary and he did not know if he would still be there when I was next in Khartoum.

'My family have written from Juba,' he said. 'They want me to leave Sudan and get a job in another country so I can send them the money my brothers and sisters need for school.'

I had already been planning to give him something for looking after me but he refused the money when I handed it to him, concerned I had misinterpreted his friendship. I wrote down my address in Scotland when he asked for it and he folded the paper neatly and placed it in his pocket as if I had given him something more precious. A minute later I was called by the driver to climb aboard. The bus was full and ready to leave.

There was still some heat left in the day as we left Khartoum. I soon lost sight of John in the billowing clouds of dust stirred by our passage, and when I looked back through the rear window, he was gone. For a moment I caught sight of the thin thread of river that flowed through the city, and the hills of sand and stone that rose on either side of it. The Nile seemed impossibly fragile in that landscape and for a moment I had a feeling of panic, remembering stories about people lost in the desert, about their terrible deaths from thirst and starvation. In just a few days the city had grown familiar and I was apprehensive about leaving it and my only friend in the whole of the country.

Jolted by the bus bouncing over pot holes I looked around. Everyone about me, men, women and children, had wrapped their shawls around their heads. All that could be seen of their faces were hooded eyes as they settled into their seats for the uncomfortable few days ahead. I felt out of place and unprepared and, not for the last time, wondered if I had made the right decision. Having abandoned friends and family and studies in Europe in favour of travel, was my choice of Africa the right one?

A passenger beside me reached inside his bag and pulled out a scarf. Without a word he handed it across and showed me how to wind it around my head, over my nose and mouth in such a way that there was space enough to breathe although the dust was kept out. A short while later someone else offered tea.

Their kindness made me feel more at ease and reduced my apprehension about the immediate future. It seemed I was not quite alone in this strange place after all. I had been handed over not to a set of strangers but to another group of people who would look after me, who would make sure I came to no harm, Inshallah.

2

Settling in

As John predicted, the northern bus struggled and bumped for two days along the track. I lost count of the number of times we had to get out, push from behind and dig the sand away from the tyres. At the time I did not know that this was the most reliable form of transport across the desert and the best way of entering the town.

After the long, uncomfortable journey Dongola appeared before us like some fabulous oasis. There were houses and trees, the Nile itself, a cool breeze coming from that direction and men, women and children waving at us as if we had just completed a journey of several weeks rather than a few days.

Some time before the town appeared we had guessed it was close when we caught the scent of the river. Moistness in the air carried with it the smell of palm trees and vegetation. That smell disappeared the moment we arrived as if it required the dust of the desert to define it, the landscape we had ploughed through to make it noticeable by contrast.

In the government run 'Rest House' to which I was directed, my new colleague, Arthur, greeted me. He was one of two teachers who had arrived in Dongola a week earlier. Like me they had not been smart enough to raise their hands when the same official in Khartoum asked who in their group knew where they wanted to be posted. He was from Leeds and had never been to Sudan or, for that matter, Africa before. Several years older than I, slightly intimidating behind a pair of thick spectacles, he looked every inch the teacher, but he had a taste for 'adventure' and was looking for an appropriate backdrop for the novel he hoped to write.

John was younger. He had just completed his studies at

Oxford and had decided to take a year off before returning to work in his father's business.

'So what's it like here?' I asked.

'Very hot,' John replied, looking up from behind his book and uttering these words as if they were the only ones he could find to describe our new location. I remembered the other John's remarks when I first told him where I was to be posted, the same words that he had used.

Arthur handed me a glass of water from the fridge that gurgled away in a corner of the room, as if it could answer my question more eloquently than any words he might find. In fact it was the first cool water I had drunk in days, something I had dreamed about during the entire journey northwards.

'And school?' I asked. 'What's that like?'

'We don't know yet,' John replied. 'Every time we present ourselves to the Ministry of Education they tell us that term hasn't started, that we should come the next day to find out.'

They both seemed friendly enough and, despite the frustration of being here without making any progress, still untouched by the cynicism I had seen among some of my colleagues earlier. I liked them. They seemed determined to accept the same advice I had been given in London, to abandon their preconceptions and keep an open mind.

Later that day Arthur approached me. 'We've managed to locate a house for rent but it's too big for two people. We'd like you to join us, if you're interested.' Glad I had been accepted, I readily agreed.

I was eager to explore my new surroundings and find out about the town, but Arthur warned me that in the heat of the day no one did anything. 'Better to wait until late afternoon when it cools down. That's when the inhabitants come out.'

Life in Dongola during the summer months began with the call to prayer just before sunrise. At mid-day most people retreated indoors to find shade and to sleep. Just before sunset everyone was back on the streets again where they would walk around, converse, meet neighbours and friends and enjoy the relative cool that the evening brought with it. The final call to prayer around nine o'clock signalled the end of the day and the return of people to their homes.

Later that afternoon Arthur and John took me on my first tour. As we walked along Dongola's narrow streets, between houses and buildings that had been coloured in white paint and plaster, we received the same friendly stares and open curiosity as in Khartoum. The groups of children who trailed behind us chanted the word 'Khawaja', translated by my dictionary as 'a term used to denote a person of foreign or European descent'. It was not said unkindly or delivered in a tone of derision but was constantly repeated as if they had to remind each other they were witnessing something remarkable.

A few men came over to shake hands and exchange a few words. We replied to their greetings in poor Arabic but despite their amusement our attempts at a few words of their language seemed to please them. 'News of English teachers from abroad has prefigured our arrival,' said Arthur. 'Ever since we've been here people have come to welcome us.'

Over and above the friends they had made, Arthur and John had also established their first hang-out in a small café on the edge of town. This provided the best view of the Nile that fronted one side of Dongola. It was my first, clear sight of the river since I had arrived and contrasted with the desert environment stretching for miles around us, it retained the same fragile and precious quality I had remarked in Khartoum.

'Café' was something of a misnomer for a small wooden shack with a tin roof and a few scattered tables and chairs. I must have looked sceptical because Arthur reassured me that it came highly recommended and that it served the best coffee in the province.

'This is our new teacher from Scotland,' was how I was introduced to Hassan, the short, plump and friendly proprietor. The coffee had a rich, powerful odour flavoured with ginger and was served in small, delicate cups decorated with Arabic calligraphy. As Arthur promised, the taste of the coffee merited its reputation but I was not prepared for the hit it delivered, the rush of caffeine that would keep me awake through most of that night.

Hassan sat beside us. Complimenting him on his coffee I said it was strong, and that I couldn't drink any more. 'Coffee is like alcohol for us,' he joked, and went on to say that beer, whisky and other spirits were rarely consumed in a part of the country where Islam was taken seriously. 'At least not in public,' he added, but there was a strong, local spirit made from dates.

'Araki' was very rough, he warned, and proceeded to tell us how he occasionally used it to light his lamps. 'Best not to drink it,' was the advice he offered.

'Why would we need to if we have your coffee?' I replied.

On the many occasions we were to visit, Hassan rarely charged us for what we consumed or the long periods of time we spent in his café. We had to press him to accept any payment. With the sun setting over the river and the cool breeze, the sight of the feluccas with their white sails, the affable greetings thrown in our direction by the men and women passing by on their donkeys, I could understand why Arthur and John had chosen this as their favourite location

'You have come here to teach our children,' Hassan said on that first evening when I asked him how much we owed. 'It would be wrong of me to make you pay.'

At the Ministry offices the next day we were informed that term had still not been announced in Khartoum and that we would have to wait to find out which school we would be posted to.

'When might that be?' I enquired from an official who barely stirred from behind his newspaper and to whom Arthur and John could no longer speak without raising their voices.

After 'Inshallah' the second most popular word in Sudan is 'Bukra,' which in my well thumbed Sudanese-Arabic to English dictionary was translated as 'tomorrow'. I was subsequently to discard that book as being unable to capture the real meaning of certain popular words.

'Bukra,' as it turned out, could denote any time in the future. This included 'tomorrow' but also the day after that, the following week or even the next month. Hassan told us that the Sudanese fear of predicting the future, of tempting fate by claiming that something would happen at a particular time, gave the word a quality of uncertainty that was probably not captured in our English translation. Combined with the expression 'Inshallah,' as in the message we had just received, 'School will open bukra, Inshallah,' it meant 'God only knows'.

Ultimately, the official was telling us that we should not be surprised by any delay since we had been warned not to have expectations.

The fact that 'tomorrow' was always an option, however, meant that every day we had to trek the considerable distance to the Ministry of Education office to learn if any progress had been made. We began to worry that schools might never open, and that this was all a scam, that someone, somewhere had duped a group of unemployed teachers in Britain to come to Sudan in expectation of work that would never materialize. Would our solidarity with children who needed to learn English ever be realized?

'And what about the salary?' John added. 'Do you realize we are getting paid for just sitting around?'

One day, a week after I arrived, two weeks after Arthur and John had been here, the same official announced that school would 'definitely' start tomorrow.

'No, not bukra,' he said, with a conviction that had been noticeably absent before, 'but tomorrow for real. Do you have a preference for the Girl's Secondary School or the Boy's Secondary School?'

Only half believing that our wait was finally coming to an end Arthur indicated he was happy to be placed anywhere, 'even if it's in the middle of the desert.'

Half an hour later I received a letter, stamped by the provincial Director of Education, announcing my appointment as English Teacher for Dongola Girls' Secondary School. Arthur and John were posted to the boys' school. 'Lucky sod,' they said, when they saw my paper, and I reminded them again they had declined to indicate any preference. After my failure in Khartoum to stick my hand up I had learned a lesson. Next day, armed with my letter and textbooks, I arrived at the school building at the appointed time of 6.30 in the morning.

'Is this the right place?' I wondered. The gates were closed and there was no sign of any teachers or pupils. I found a solitary guard, who informed me that school had not yet started and that I should try again the following week.

'Are you sure?' I asked. 'I have this piece of paper.'

Not even bothering to look he ushered me away and told me that a piece of paper was not enough to open his school. 'Come back next week,' he repeated. 'Maybe we will be open then.'

Arthur and John had a similar encounter. 'Don't worry,' the official in the Ministry replied when confronted by three irate teachers later that morning. 'The pupils will turn up soon enough. Did you expect schools to open today when we only announced the start of term yesterday?'

'We've time to kill,' said John. 'So what shall we do now?'

In a new town in a strange country, with new people around us and in an environment that was unfamiliar, that question soon answered itself. In Arthur's 'A Travellers Guide to Sudan' I read that Dongola was a relatively recent settlement, founded in 1811 by an invading Mameluk army of Turks and Egyptians. They had burned the old capital to the ground, and established their new outpost on the Nile some sixty kilometres to the north.

The town was sometimes referred to as 'Dongola Jadid' (new Dongola) and was famous for dates, fish and the ruins of an ancient Pharonic settlement on the east bank of the river at a place called Kawa. There was some evidence that Roman legions had also penetrated this far down the Nile. The population was estimated at between eighteen to twenty thousand people, and even though we didn't need reminding: 'Temperatures in this part of the country are very high.'

Like other settlements in Sudan, Dongola was structured

around a central market. From there the streets radiated outwards with the cafés, mosques, municipal buildings and Government offices congregated around it. On Wednesdays and Saturdays the streets nearest the market were almost impassable, full of people making their way to the scores of stalls and shops that sold produce from all over the province.

'Markets,' said our guide book, 'are the heart and soul of all settlements in Sudan.' Observing people about their business, the enthusiasm and excitement that seized the entire population during these days, I could see what this meant. It was like stepping back in time. Our own commerce and trade would once have taken place in these kinds of locations, before the purchase of goods and services became more sanitized and formal. It wasn't only buying and selling that took place. There were street performers, religious men in strange robes reciting the Koran, beggars and street urchins, cafés and restaurants full of people, everyone using the opportunity to exchange news and gossip, to celebrate the pleasure the Sudanese obviously took in each other's company.

There was pretty much everything on offer during market days in Dongola. There were stalls offering camel and goat meat, vegetables and a bewildering variety of herbs and spices, large mounds of dates that the province exported all over the country. When I first attempted to buy some I was asked by the vendor which one of the twenty plus varieties he had on sale I wanted. Clueless as to what the difference between them might be I shrugged my shoulders and asked him to give me whatever he thought I would most like.

Another corner of the market was reserved for livestock: camels, goats and a shaggy kind of sheep that managed to survive in the harsh conditions of the province. Also on sale were donkeys, including the sturdy, white animals the official in Khartoum had referred to when he told me where I was to be posted. The Dongola donkey was famous throughout the country and beyond. Truth to tell I could hardly distinguish it from the other donkeys that sold for considerably less. Hassan, our community guide as well as provider of fine coffee, informed us that a good animal could fetch over a thousand dollars, 'not Sudanese dollars but real United States dollars,' from buyers who came from as far away as Egypt, Libya and even Pakistan to find them.

'What makes them so special?' I asked.

'Ride a bicycle. Then ride a motorcycle,' he replied. 'You'll know what the difference is then.'

It was not only local produce that was on offer. There were Sony radios and televisions, water pumps made in China, car parts that seemed out of place beside the camels and goats they shared a space with. Some stalls sold expensive cloth from India, displaying a wide variety of colourful saris, called Tobes, which Sudanese women would wrap around themselves whenever they appeared in public.

The best place to experience the market was from one of the coffee shops on the edge of the square. We would sit and watch for several hours the interactions between people, the arguments and joking, the play-acting that seemed to accompany every trade, the inevitable cup of tea or coffee shared after a deal was struck. Unaccustomed to haggling ourselves, we generally agreed to the prices asked by the vendors.

'No,' said Hassan. 'You are supposed to quarrel about the price. No trader can feel satisfied unless you have had an argument. Offer them a quarter of what they ask for,' he advised, 'and if you agree on a half then everyone should be happy.'

Apart from the central market and the small harbour on the river where the boats tied up, two other landmarks in town were the large, imposing mosque a few streets away and, directly opposite it, the local cinema. They confronted each other in the same way that public houses and churches stand uneasily together in Scotland.

As Hassan had said, alcohol was only rarely consumed in northern Sudan, and never openly. There were no bars, pubs or discos, so apart from the cafés where they regularly hung out, the only place for young men with energy to burn in the evenings was the cinema. In full view of the most religious establishment in town there was nothing discreet about it.

Displayed on its walls for all to see were large posters advertising the latest films, generally displaying women in varying states of undress, with pouting lips, preposterous bosoms and a sexual suggestiveness I would never have expected in this location.

'Shall we go?' John suggested one evening, when full of energy ourselves we had drawn a blank as to where we could find other entertainment.

There was a long queue when we arrived, considerable noise and anticipation, and vendors selling popcorn, fried beans and fizzy drinks. Powered by a generator which drowned the voices coming over the loudspeaker, the film was projected on to a wall that had more holes and dark patches than white paint.

The real entertainment, however, was not the Kung Fu films or the outdated movies from Hollywood. It was the audience itself that provided the more interesting spectacle. Largely comprised of young men, with a few families tucked away in a corner, they were noisy, loud and easily amused. Every time the hero of the film was threatened or beaten up, the whistling and jeering would begin. When the bad guys were shot the audience erupted in cheering. The most enthusiastic applause took place whenever one of the ladies revealed more flesh than would have been appropriate in a community where women never showed more than a discreet ankle in public. When half a bosom was exposed the crowd went wild.

'Is it true that women behave like this in your country?' a group of young men asked us during a break in the film. The question seemed less censorious than wistful, as if they were anxious about what they might be missing.

They seemed disappointed to hear that this was not the case, that if someone appeared half naked in public we would have been as surprised as if we had seen it on the streets of Dongola. 'But in most of the films we see, the women seem to lose their clothes very easily,' one of them insisted, as if we had upset a cherished myth and distorted a feature of the communities we came from.

Of the mosque itself that cast a long shadow over the goings on in the cinema beside it every Friday and Saturday evening, we saw very little.

'Are you a Muslim?' the guard at the gate confronted me when I tried to enter one day. I shook my head.

'No Masahi in here,' he replied, the word in Sudan that was used for Christians. As I was to discover, this rule was not uniformly applied throughout the province. If you removed your shoes and were dressed in a respectful manner, the guards at the gate would sometimes relent and let you in.

A few days after we moved into our new house, there was a banging at the door. Outside was a man with glasses, wearing a traditional white gown and headdress, and behind him a retinue of young children carrying trays. Khalid turned out to be our next door neighbour, come to welcome us with a traditional Sudanese meal of beans, goat meat, a type of stringy vegetable called 'lady's fingers', dates from his orchard and Coca Cola.

As we ate, the children clustered around us in obvious fascination. There were no forks and knives and we had not yet mastered the technique of using our hands. Whenever we succeeded in consuming a mouthful of food without it dribbling down our chins they politely applauded. Hassan chatted away, his English better than our Arabic. Though not presented in a boastful way it became clear he was one of the richest merchants in town. He bought and sold dates, spices and dried fish, had a fleet of trucks to transport goods throughout the country, and owned several houses in different parts of Sudan. He had three wives and fifteen children, five of them standing in front of us.

Somehow the conversation got round to the subject of religion and in particular Arthur's irritation at being woken up every morning at five o'clock when the call to prayer came booming through our streets. Only a few blocks away from the mosque we could not fail to hear it broadcast five times a day. Half joking Arthur said, 'If I ever meet the person who wakes me up I'll pick an argument and tell him to keep his voice down.'

Khalid laughed. 'Then I'm the one you're looking for,' he said. His family had been 'muezzins' for several generations. He had learnt the skill from his father, who in turn had been taught by his father. The noise that Arthur thought was 'a nuisance' was a recitation from the Koran that had to be delivered in just the right way. There was a critical audience in Dongola, Khalid continued, and if he got it wrong he would soon know about it. 'I'll try to keep my voice down next time, though,' he added, while the children around us erupted in giggles at Arthur's obvious embarrassment.

The house we had moved into in the central area of town turned out to be fairly typical, built to a pattern that rarely varied throughout the province. Although there may have been differences in the size of households and the quality of building materials (bricks, cement, tiled roofs in the smarter suburbs of Dongola; wood, mud and thatch in the poorer areas), the fundamental plan remained the same.

There was the inevitable high wall to keep out the prying eyes of strangers. 'Privacy is highly valued in this part of the country,' Khalid explained, 'No one wants the women of the family exposed to the curiosity of outsiders.'

The rooms were generally constructed around a central courtyard, usually an open space with a tree to provide shade from the sun. The men's and women's quarters were always separated. Away from the kitchen, which was where the women spent much of their time, was the best room of the house, the place where guests and visitors were entertained. As we discovered, it was possible to visit someone's house, to be served a meal, to be entertained for several hours, even to sleep overnight, and never catch a glimpse of the women who did all the work. This segregation of the sexes determined the use of space in many of the houses we visited, no matter the economic status of the family.

There was no municipal electricity supply in Dongola when we arrived, but there were rumours this was about to change with the construction of an electricity plant on the outskirts of town, but even those who spoke about it weren't holding their

breath. This rumour had been circulating for almost a decade.
Most people used charcoal for cooking and paraffin for their
lamps. A few of the wealthier families had their own small
generators. Every evening just after sunset the silence of the
neighbourhood would be shattered by the sound of machines
starting up, including Khalid's next door.

Our house had a tap in the courtyard but this never emitted
more than a thin, irregular trickle. Khalid introduced us to the
local water-carrier when we first moved in, a thin man with a
ragged donkey who for a few Sudanese shillings would fetch
several buckets from a well nearby. The fact that we paid for
each cupful, combined with the general scarcity of water in the
town (despite the proximity of one of Africa's longest rivers),
taught us a level of frugality that would be inconceivable in
Scotland where water is as common as air. Care not to waste
such a valuable commodity was part of a strong, local tradition, and probably a necessity in a desert environment where it
could make the difference between death and survival. I once
saw Khalid severely scold his twelve-year-old son for having
spilled no more than a few drops from the cup he was carrying,
as if it were whisky or an expensive wine.

Without electricity and a fridge we were concerned about
the temperature of the water, especially during the heat of the
day when Arthur's thermometer touched 45 Celsius. Khalid
offered to take us to a small 'factory' on the edge of the town
where rows and rows of red pots had been set out to bake in
the sun. We bought four large jars, called 'Zirs', and some
metal stands they fitted into that kept them suspended a few
feet above the ground.

'What good will these do?' I wondered aloud.

When filled, the porous clay oozed slow, steady moisture
that evaporated in the heat. After an hour or so we had cool
water and a container where you could keep food wrapped in
plastic for a few hours longer than the temperature would
otherwise have allowed.

Our toilet was a raised, concrete block in a corner of the
courtyard with some thatch around it for privacy and a hole in

the middle to squat over. George had already warned us what to expect, telling us that the luxury of a raised, flushable loo made of white porcelain was only available in the smartest hotels in Khartoum. Toilet paper was not on sale either and so we became quickly familiar with the custom of using our left hands to clean ourselves. Our guide-book warned us of the anger that might be caused if we ever dipped that same hand into any food that was offered, or extended it in greeting to anyone in the country. John had to make a special effort not to cause offence, since he was naturally left handed.

'Where does the waste from the toilet go?' Arthur asked Khalid when he first visited.

He told us that the bucket beneath the hole would be emptied once a week by men driving around in a truck for just that purpose. We were not to be alarmed if we saw them. Their faces would be completely covered and their bodies wrapped in a variety of old rags to make sure that no part of them would be exposed. They would drive around in their truck at some early hour when everyone was asleep, he added.

'But if you are awake the smell of their arrival will be as noticeable as the noise of their vehicle pulling up on the road outside.'

'But what happens to the waste?' Arthur continued, with a persistence I felt was hardly prudent. There are some things it is best not to ask about.

'It is used for fertilizer,' Khalid replied. 'Why do you think the tomatoes you have been eating are so big?'

3

Learning about each other

Abdel-Majid was head of the English department, which consisted of himself and no one else.

He was a tall, thin man with thick spectacles that made him look older than his years. As it turned out he was the same age as me. Fresh out of college in Khartoum this was his first job as a teacher. Perhaps this made him nervous, but he had a real vocation and wanted to prove himself in his new post. Desperate to have someone share the burden of teaching English, he was effusive in his welcome when we finally met a week after term officially started.

'Since you are an expert you can have the most difficult class,' he said.

'I don't have that much experience, Abdel-Majid.'

'How many years have you been a teacher? Two, three . . . more?'

'Only a few months,' I was reluctant to admit that my only experience had been teaching rich Spanish children for several weeks when I was a student.

'That's okay,' he replied, as if probing for some redeeming quality. 'We need a native speaker to teach the girls proper pronunciation. Soon they will all be speaking like those people we hear on the BBC World Service.'

Apologetically I pointed out that I came from the north of Scotland. 'Unfortunately we don't do BBC English in that part of the country.'

I felt his English was better than my own. Clearer, slower, it would be easier for pupils in the 'difficult' class to understand. In the end we agreed on a compromise. We would share the most difficult class as well as the easy one, but to start with I would be given the latter.

George had warned us that classes of fifty to sixty students were common, and that there would be no text books, pencils or paper, perhaps not even a blackboard to draw on. As it turned out I was introduced to a group of about twenty girls, all of whom had pens and paper and enough text-books to share. When they looked up at me with curious, open faces I felt that I had fallen on my feet.

That evening Arthur told me he had also been lucky. 'With only fifteen boys in my class, work will be a dawdle,' he said. John had also done well with a group of twenty-two students. Something was not quite right, I suspected, or maybe George had been more cynical than I imagined.

The next day my group of girls had swelled considerably and soon, by the end of the week, I counted fifty-five and numbers still rising.

Abdel-Majid told me that it took time for word to spread around the province. 'Some pupils have to travel from as far away as Khartoum, since there are no school places available for them in the capital. Coming to a remote location like this is the only way to continue their education.'

The initial, polite silence that first greeted me when I entered the classroom soon degenerated into a babble of noise and distraction. I politely asked the girls to quieten down. After a few embarrassed giggles the chatter resumed, and raising my voice didn't help. The headmaster, a balding, serious man who seemed to have the weight of the world on his shoulders, took me aside one day and asked why I couldn't keep them under control.

'If you can't keep discipline, send them to the soldier out-side,' he said, pointing to a large man of military bearing who prowled the premises with a long, wooden stick. I had as-sumed he was one of the school guards.

I confided to Abdel-Majid that I hadn't been too fond of discipline at my own school and hadn't come all the way to Sudan to send children out of my class for a beating.

'If you don't send a clear message now,' he replied, 'the girls will only take advantage. Word will soon get around that you can't keep control. Remember this is the easy class. What will you do with the difficult one?'

His face had a look that said, 'Why have I been sent someone who is no help to me at all?' I refrained from telling him that not only had I consistently irked my teachers but I had also been suspended on several occasions. The school authorities had seen me as something of a troublemaker.

'You'll never come to any good, McIvor,' was an expression frequently tossed in my direction, including by my former headmaster who, balding, serious, and with the same air of bearing a weighty burden, reminded me of his counterpart here in Dongola. There was no question of calling on the services of the soldier. But some solution had to be found. My professional reputation was at stake.

On one of the few occasions when the girls quietened down, I asked them why they showed so little interest in learning English. Didn't they think it was a shame that their Government had paid scarce money to bring me all the way from Scotland (they knew where it was because I had drawn them a map) only to waste my time?

'What would your parents say if they knew you were wasting your time too?' I asked.

One of the more confident girls stood up. 'What's the point in being educated if your parents tell you to get married at the end of it and your husband doesn't let you get a job?'

'We're only here to increase our bride price,' confided another, going on to explain that a girl who had several years of schooling behind her was worth more when she got married. Growing more confident by the minute the girls who had rarely spoken in my class, in English at least, also begin to contribute.

'Only a small number of students ever pass their final exams, so what's the point in working hard if most of us will fail?'

'These are the years when we are supposed to have fun,' said a fourth. 'When you're older and have children fun stops.'

Despite the mispronunciations and erratic grammar all these points had been delivered in a quality of English I had not heard in my class before. They had also been said amid a silence that indicated everyone's engagement. I suddenly realized that maybe the text books I had been given were as boring to listen to as they were to teach. Maybe if I could involve the students in things that interested them, I would have a chance of improving their language skills. Maybe the noise and chatter would die down too and that look of concern on Abdel-Majid's face every time I met him would lighten.

I suggested a compromise. The reader that would feature in the national end of term exams was an inappropriate play about 19th century English manners called, 'The Importance of Being Earnest' by George Bernard Shaw. Half the time we would focus on this but, in return for their concentration and effort, we would spend the rest of the class in discussing whatever topic was of interest to them. So long as I was allowed to correct their grammar and pronunciation while they were speaking, no subject was out of bounds. The girls consulted among themselves for a few minutes and elected a spokesperson.

'The first thing we want to talk about,' she said, 'is whether women drink alcohol and smoke cigarettes in Scotland. And is it true that they can choose their husbands for themselves, even without the agreement of their parents?'

Abdel-Majid took me aside a few days later, a look of genuine appreciation on his face. 'What did you do with the girls?' he enquired.

The headmaster had remarked on a noticeable improvement in the levels of noise coming from my class. He wanted to know how I had managed to turn a group of unruly students into model pupils without recourse to the 'soldier'. The other teachers were intrigued too. Maybe this was a technique they could learn from, Abdel-Majid suggested.

I shrugged my shoulders and said nothing. Part of the deal with the girls was that whenever the headmaster or another teacher approached they were to bury their heads in their text books and pretend interest. I did not want to reveal the full extent to which we ignored most of the curriculum. Enthused by the topics that featured in our discussions my students, for the moment at least, had not let on either.

Most of the girls came from outside Dongola and resided in basic premises inside the school grounds. In a society where until recently they were expected to stay at home, get married and have children at a young age, education for them was not without controversy.

'We are never allowed out of this place,' they would complain, pointing out that for girls to live away from home before they were married was opposed by some in their communities. As if to answer their concerns the school was surrounded by a wall with bits of glass on top like sharp teeth. It was high enough, not only to keep the girls inside but also to prevent the eyes of the outside world from looking in.

'Why are some people opposed to your education?' I asked.

'They think that we will come to no good,' replied one girl, 'that we will learn things that will undermine our traditions.'

'They think that education will make us unhappy with what we have, that we will expect more for ourselves than having children, looking after our husbands, cooking food and washing dishes,' volunteered another.

'Some men are uncomfortable with women standing up for themselves and questioning their behaviour. They say that education will make us bad wives. But if we are educated, won't our children be better educated too?'

Not withstanding the high wall that surrounded them, the girls had to wear shawls and scarves the whole time. They did not conceal their faces completely, like women who wore the Burkah in some other Muslim societies, but a glimpse of a woman's hair was regarded as provocative and no one from outside the family should ever be allowed to see it, including their teachers. Basketball practice, which took place after school hours in the early evening when it was cooler, became an exercise in keeping their scarves around their heads while engaged in vigorous effort at the same time.

Fatima, who came from Atbara, a town a few hundred kilometres north of Khartoum, was one of the smartest girls in the school. A bright fifteen-year-old she constantly asked me searching questions about English grammar. 'My parents only agreed to my continuing education on condition I would not speak to boys or go to public places without a family member present,' she told me.

None of the girls, despite their complaints about being bored and not being allowed outside for weeks on end, thought this unfair. I asked them why. The sight of an uncovered woman or a teenage girl was a distraction to men, they replied, which prevented them from carrying out their duties and responsibilities. Far from being the man's fault, the blame lay with the woman who had 'provoked' him.

According to the girls, when it came to relationships with women, men were inherently weak, easily distracted and unable to control themselves. 'So it is our responsibility not to distract them,' one of the girls explained.

'What about me?' I asked. 'I haven't lost control standing here in front of sixty young girls. Nor have your other teachers.'

'That's because we are appropriately dressed,' Fatima interjected. 'Girls who wear inappropriate clothes, smoke cigarettes and speak to boys in public are asking for trouble. They are the ones who are doing wrong.'

'Women in Scotland don't wear headscarves and some of them smoke cigarettes,' I replied. 'Are you saying they deserve to be punished?'

'No,' she said. 'It's different for women in your part of the world.'

'Why?'

'They're not Muslim. We expect them to behave badly. Our brothers have told us what they see in the cinema every week, about the behaviour of women in your country. If they were Muslim it would be different, such behaviour would not be tolerated.'

The other girls nodded in agreement. But against what seemed to be a sincerely held view, their curiosity about

Western fashion and customs intrigued me. They displayed an eager interest in how men and women interacted in other societies and seemed envious when I told them that many women in Scotland continued to work after marriage, and that their choice of husband was their own. When I told them that household duties were often shared between men and women and that my mother had expected me to do my share of the housework and wash the dishes when I was a boy, they looked at each other and laughed. Later, I discovered they had leaked this information to other teachers in the school, as if I had confided some scandalous family secret.

Within a month of my arrival in Dongola I was speaking Arabic with some fluency. This was partly due to the fact that very little English was spoken in town, leaving me no choice but to make an effort to acquire the language. I also realized that gaining any level of meaningful insight into the lives of the people around me would depend on my ability to communicate with them, to move beyond the standard greetings and expressions I had acquired in my first week in the country. But there were other, more pressing reasons for understanding what was going on.

One day Abdel-Majid informed me that my hair needed to be cut, that the headmaster had remarked that I looked untidy and should project a more 'respectable' image to the girls. 'Besides, what's the point in having long hair in a climate that is hot enough already?'

He pointed me towards a number of barber shops in town. None of the ones I visited boasted anything more than a wooden seat and a person with a pair of scissors and a sharp razor. There were no mirrors on the walls either, to let you know what was going on.

'I only want a trim,' was what I thought I said. But whether this was interpreted as 'Take it all off,' or whether the barber decided that he knew what was in my own best interests, I emerged on to the streets of Dongola with a shaven head.

Arthur and John were scathing and did nothing to reassure me that I did not look a complete idiot. Abdel-Majid grinned and claimed he had not demanded anything so severe. 'You'll have to improve your language skills if you want a better cut next time.'

'Why don't you wear a headscarf?' was the advice the girls offered when they saw me. Next day one of them produced a long roll of white cotton. They showed me how to wrap it around my head and then stood back to admire their handiwork.

'Now you look better,' they agreed, and suggested that I should consider wearing a jellabiya like the other teachers.

I laughed, thinking it was a joke, imagining the derision that would greet me in Dongola if I were ever so foolish as to do so.

'Why not,' they persisted. 'Aren't the shirts, ties, trousers and shoes you wear uncomfortable in this heat?'

I shrugged my shoulders, still suspicious.

'When Sudanese visit your country,' someone else argued, 'they wear what you wear, don't they? So why don't Europeans do the same when they come here? There is no shame in putting them on.'

Abdel-Majid concurred but offered an additional insight. 'Some people here will think it strange; that is true. They may stare at you. But this is not because they will be offended or because they think you are fooling around. It's just that so many Europeans have never made the effort to adapt to our country, either to speak our language or dress like we do. They would prefer to remain uncomfortable than to believe they are losing face.'

I pondered this. As the girls had said, the local clothes were appropriate for the climate. They seemed comfortable and were not without a certain elegance and style, but some part of me felt that appearing in public with them on, would mean abandoning some part of my own culture and that I would be losing part of my identity. It might start with a change of clothes, but where would it end?

I remembered George's dismissive remarks about one of the teachers he had known when he first came to Sudan, about how he had 'gone native'. Other colleagues had nodded their heads in condemnation as if this were one of the worst things that could befall an Englishman (or Scotsman) working in a foreign country. While it might be okay to teach, to offer help, to show some occasional solidarity, there was a line that must never be crossed. Accepting a local tradition was like abandoning your own.

In the end it came down to the heat and a sense that I would lose nothing more than my prejudice that convinced me to buy some local clothes. Abdel-Majid took me to his tailor on the edge of the market and a week later they were ready. When I appeared on the streets of the town no one turned to stare or laugh. Hassan served me coffee in exactly the same way he had done since I started visiting his establishment. In school the girls remarked how comfortable I looked. I wondered what all the fuss had been about and the hollowness of my initial reservations.

With lessons finishing at mid-day and with little to entertain them in the dreary confines of the school grounds the girls suffered from boredom. Their complaints reached the headmaster who told us to organize some extra-curricular activities.

One day, a small delegation of students approached me to request my attendance at one of the evening classes that had been organized in the wake of this instruction. I had once mentioned that I had brought a guitar with me from Scotland and they were interested to hear me play. 'We have never seen a guitar before.'

I pointed out that I had only just started to learn, that I only knew one song and was hardly in a position to entertain them, but they insisted. 'It will be an opportunity to talk to us about music in Scotland and you can correct our grammar at the same time.'

On the date that had been agreed I noticed some activity in the school grounds around the raised concrete block that would serve as a stage. Another teacher told me that there would be a concert that evening and some local musicians were expected. Since it would start directly after the evening classes, I decided to attend, eager to hear Sudanese music for the first time.

The guitar was a success. The girls crowded around, asked sensible questions in English and leafed through a copy of 'Learning to Play the Guitar in Twenty Easy Lessons'. They even managed to tease out the names of various rock stars I had once hoped to emulate. Deep in our discussion an announcement came over the loud speakers that had been set up outside. A moment later Abdel-Majid appeared and told me that it was time for me to perform.

'I just did,' I said. 'Look.' The girls were still clustered around the instrument and eagerly inspecting the book I had brought with me.

He laughed. 'Not to the people outside you haven't. Everyone's waiting for you to begin.'

I was familiar enough with him by then to know when he was serious and when he was having fun. This time he was not joking. I began to panic.

'Who said I could play the guitar, Abdel-Majid? I know only one song.'

'They did,' he replied, pointing to the girls who had gone silent in the classroom.

'Well I can't and never told anyone I could. You'd better tell the people who have gathered outside, to listen to someone else.' I was determined above all not to make a fool of myself.

Abdel-Majid left but returned later with an irate headmaster.

'Many parents have come to hear you play,' he said severely. 'They understand you are very talented.' Memories of my headmaster in secondary school in Scotland welled up, the kind of person you never argued with or ever wanted to get on the wrong side of.

'Excuse me, Sir, but I never told anyone any such thing. How can I go out there when I don't even know how to play the instrument?'

'If you make the effort I'm sure it will be appreciated by everyone,' he replied, ignoring what I had just said. 'Your best is good enough for us.' I could see there was little point in arguing further.

By then a considerable crowd had gathered: pupils, teachers, parents, other members of the community I recognized. Perhaps if I told them the truth, I thought, if I explained to them that it had all been a terrible mistake I would be let off the hook. But the moment I got up on stage an enthusiastic round of applause began. This became even louder when I announced over the loudspeaker that I was not very good, that I had only started to play the guitar a few weeks ago, and that my voice was fine for teaching but not for singing. A public acknowledgement of incompetence had been interpreted as a gesture of humility, the words of someone trying to be coy about their talents. I felt like a fly caught in a web where the more you struggle the more entangled you become, and the more impossible it is to escape.

In the end I played my one song over and over, trying to vary the chords so that it would come out different every time. I also managed a rendition of 'Flower of Scotland,' making up the words I had forgotten. I was thankful for the darkness of the evening which concealed my embarrassment, and the poor sound system I could later blame for my appalling performance. I stepped down to a round of polite but noticeably muted applause, clearly not having lived up to expectations.

The girls from the evening class seemed amused, huddled together and giggling as I walked past them. I wondered if this had been a set up, some entertainment organized at my expense to help relieve the boredom of their lives at school.

'At least you tried,' Abdel-Majid consoled me as I went to the back of the stage where he was waiting. 'With a bit of practice you'll be fine next time. When do you think you will play again?'

'Bukra,' I said emphatically, not meaning 'tomorrow', 'next week' or even 'next year'. This time the word definitely meant 'never'.

4

Along the banks of the Nile

Along the banks of the Nile it is difficult to say where one community ends and another begins. A ribbon of settlement traces much of the river, thicker in places, thinner in others, but rarely empty of villages and households completely. Without the water, of course, none of this would be possible.

The other essential components that have enabled settlement in an inhospitable environment are the palm trees, ubiquitous throughout the communities of northern Sudan.

The villagers point to their plantations with considerable pride, and are able to tell you when individual trees were planted and by whom. Not only do they provide wood for their homes, thatch to cover their roofs and floors, dates for consumption and export, but palm trees also anchor the mud deposited by the river around their roots. Without them that precious soil would be washed away.

'There is nothing that grows in this part of the country without a palm tree close by,' Abdel-Majid told me. He added that many of the images carved on the walls of the pyramids scattered along the Nile and the decorations painted on more contemporary houses indicate the reverence in which they have always been held. This attitude of the people towards their trees left me thinking of the more dismissive and cavalier attitude found in our own culture towards the environment in which we live, our profligacy when it comes to the resources on which we depend.

Friday was our day off from school. As the novelty and distraction of the market began to wear off I became more adventurous and my range of exploration increased to the communities on either side of Dongola. Further out from the centre of town there was a noticeable change. It was not only the houses that looked different, built from mud and thatch rather than bricks and zinc roofs, but the people too. They were darker skinned and some of the men had facial markings. The women were ready to exchange greetings and did not conceal themselves like the women in town. The language they spoke was not the Arabic I was used to either.

Ibrahim, a teacher in our school and head of the history department, had told me he was not an Arab but a 'Dongo-lawi,' one of several groups that comprised the Nubian population of northern Sudan. When I asked him about the people outside the town, he explained that the principal settlements in the province were largely 'colonized' by Arab traders and merchants. Although they had been here for several generations they were relative newcomers to the area. The indigenous people, who had lived along the river for centuries, were the principal agriculturalists and tradesmen of the province. These were the people I was most likely to encounter the further from Dongola I ventured, he said.

The Nubians had their own languages, and while most of them converted to Islam when it spread through North Africa in the 16th Century, they jealously guarded their traditions and culture. Early Christian missionaries to the Nile Valley, sent from the eastern Roman Empire to convert them, found a population still worshipping ancient gods such as Isis and Osiris. Ibrahim went on to explain that when northern Egypt was invaded by an Assyrian army, the Pharonic kings had relocated their capital to Merowe, a town further south than Dongola. 'One of the most famous temple complexes of the Pharonic era is not in Egypt at all, but in Sudan, and the people you see depicted on the walls of these pyramids are the ancestors of the people who live here today.'

I recalled the discussion I had had with John in Khartoum when I first arrived, about ethnicity and its contribution to the conflicts that beset the country.

'There is tension here too,' Ibrahim confirmed. 'Arab merchants dominate the economy of the province. Arab farmers own the best land. The Nubians feel marginalized. It is true that relations are not as bad as in other parts of Sudan and thankfully there are no religious divisions, but conflict is there.'

He went on to say that his father was of Arab descent and could trace his family several generations back to a community in Yemen. He had married a Nubian woman from a village south of Dongola, a decision that irked members of his family who were concerned that he had married outside his social group. His father had married other wives and so Ibrahim's upbringing had largely taken place under his mother's supervision. That was why he could speak the local language and why he now called himself a Nubian. 'If you want to see how our people live you will have to go further out from town than the few miles your legs will carry you. When you leave Dongola and its suburbs behind, you will find a different community.'

I was intrigued, but in the absence of regular public transport and with only Fridays at my disposal I wondered how the world outside town could become more accessible. One evening I mentioned this to Hassan, who came up with a solution.

For the price of feeding it for the day he was prepared to lend me his donkey. He expressed his regret that he did not own the kind of pedigree animal that Dongola was famous for, but recalling his description of a speeding motorcycle I was relieved that he didn't. There was the matter of never having ridden a donkey before. But how difficult could that be, I asked myself.

'When people tell you that donkeys are stubborn,' Hassan counselled, 'then you need to believe them. These animals will try your patience. This is what you need,' he added, handing me a stick.

I did not tell him that I had no intention of administering the kind of treatment I had already witnessed in town. When donkeys refused to move or resisted the heavy loads they were made to carry, or when they decided that shade was more pleasant than the hot sun in front of them, they were soundly beaten. A gentle prod would be more than enough, I thought to myself.

As it turned out, Hassan's donkey had a mind of its own and my first few excursions occasioned considerable amusement. People were intrigued to see my efforts at persuading it to move forward. The animal, probably alert to my unwillingness to thrash it, took advantage. Nevertheless my ability to explore the surrounding area was considerably enhanced and soon the further reaches of the town, and the villages beyond, were within range.

'That animal looks tired, and so do you. Why don't you stop and have a rest?' These words were spoken one day by a middle-aged man seated under a tree along the road from Dongola. It was hot and dusty and the donkey had been acting up, sorely testing my patience.

Muglid, as it turned out, had once been an English teacher in northern Sudan. He had given that up to earn more money as a merchant in Khartoum, trading dates from the province with his contacts in other countries. Frustrated with the life of the city he had returned to farm the few acres of family land he had inherited on the death of his father. Under his tree, drinking his coffee while the world passed by, he exuded an infectious equanimity and contentment.

He ordered one of his sons to fetch some water. Another led my donkey to the shaded side of the house where four or five others were tethered. There was an eruption of noise when they confronted each other. I imagined my own animal complaining about the terrible day he had had and how I had deprived him of his day off.

'So you're the English teacher from Scotland,' Muglid continued and asked me how I liked teaching in Dongola Girls Secondary School. I wondered how he knew so much about me; my name, my country, the school where I taught.

'I confided that at first it had not been easy, that the girls had been disruptive and had not wanted to learn. 'Things are better now,' I added.

The cool water was welcome in the heat of the day. With an

irate donkey to contend with as well, I was reluctant to explore further. I wondered if I was intruding on Muglid's time but he seemed happy to practise his English. 'Would you like to see my farm?' he asked.

'Of course I would.'

Surrounded by his sons and daughters, we walked along a narrow path towards the river. The fields looked much the same, small patches of land surrounded by a raised earthen canal which channelled a steady stream of water on to the crops. There were no fences to mark them, no signs to indicate whose property we were passing through.

'There is no need,' Muglid informed me. 'Everyone knows where everyone else's land begins and ends.' He pointed to a bush in the distance and indicated that this marked the start of his neighbour's property. A clump of trees further on was the boundary of someone else's land.

Closer to the Nile we came to Muglid's fields. They were a deep green with the beans, vegetables and sorghum he had planted. There were lines of palm trees too, with clusters of dark brown dates on top of them. Despite their height, Muglid's sons scaled them with ease and threw down some dates to where we were standing.

'Yes, there are numerous varieties,' Muglid confirmed, depending on the type of tree, the time the dates were picked, how long they were stored and in what conditions. The dates from Dongola were among the most sought after and commanded the highest prices throughout North Africa.

From where we stood the river was still some distance away and I wondered how the water was transported to keep his crops irrigated. I presumed that the donkeys I had seen earlier were used for that purpose. 'Yes and no,' Muglid replied. 'We use our donkeys but in a way that is more sophisticated than you might think.'

In the centre of one of his fields was a large wooden 'machine'. It was composed of two wheels locked together, one on its side and another upright. The latter extended into a deep trench dug into the ground to a few metres, at the bottom of which was a deep pool of muddy water. One of the children tied up the donkeys to a set of harnesses. When they pushed forward the wheels began to turn and a steady stream of water poured into the nearby fields. Within a short period of time the land closest to us had been flooded.

'This has been in our family for generations,' he said. 'When one of the parts is broken we simply build another. The wood comes from our trees. The donkeys provide the energy, and the water is a gift from the river.'

He pointed to the opposite bank of the Nile which had more desert than the bank on which we were standing. Several large sand dunes ran to the edge of the water. 'On the other side of those dunes,' he said, 'is the settlement of Kawa. Have you ever been there?' I shook my head, recalling that Arthur's guidebook had mentioned there were Roman ruins in the area but I had not realized they were quite so close. 'On some of the walls of that old settlement you will see carvings of water wheels just like this one. The design hasn't changed much since that time. Why use something different when what you have is good enough?'

'Let me show you something else,' he continued, and we marched off towards some other fields. The same crops were there, the beans and vegetables and sorghum we had seen earlier. Muglid picked up some soil and crumbled it between his fingers. It seemed drier and more brittle than the rich mud on his property.

'That is what is ruining our land,' Muglid said, pointing to a wooden shed in the middle of the field with several pipes coming out of it. Inside was a pump like the ones I had seen on sale in the market.

'They are more efficient,' he continued. 'My wooden wheel and donkeys can't compete with an engine like this one, but they are inappropriate here. This machine is not what we need.'

According to Muglid, diesel pumps were becoming more common in the communities along the river. They had encouraged a form of intensive agriculture that was damaging the land at the same time. Too much water flushed the nutrients out of the soil and carried a layer of salts from deep underground that damaged their crops. Because of the number of pumps now in use the level of the water table had also fallen, forcing them to dig deeper every year.

'I am worried that soon we will only be able to find water at a level that is too deep for us to use. Then we will have no agriculture at all.'

I was curious as to why, in the face of such consequences, farmers pursued a technology that would ruin their livelihoods. 'Why don't people stop using these pumps if that is the case?' I asked Muglid. 'Why are they damaging the environment on which they depend?'

Muglid sighed in frustration. 'I used to have a pump like this one,' he replied. 'In the first few years it made me a lot of money, but then I saw that in the long term I would pay a penalty. The price would be the future of my land.'

According to Muglid, part of the problem was that Government agricultural advisors tried to convince them that their traditional technologies were backward and inefficient. '"Why are you using donkeys and primitive wooden wheels?' they would say to us. 'We are on board a bus called Progress and it is leaving you behind.'"

There were incentives offered too. Farmers would buy a pump on credit and as a gift they would receive fertilizer and seeds. The yield in the first few years would be well above normal. Happy with their profits the farmers would then buy more fertilizer and seed. After a while the land would begin to deteriorate and they would have to apply more and more chemicals just to keep up with their previous production. Increasingly in debt some of them would use their land as collateral to procure the inputs they needed to survive. 'Finally they have to sell their land to the same company that sold them their pump. By the time they see where that bus is headed it is too late to get off.'

Back at Muglid's house I found my donkey fed and watered and in a better mood for the return journey. Muglid insisted that I needed to be fed too and so I sat down with him to share a meal before my departure. I had enjoyed my stay, the frankness of the discussion and Muglid's readiness to share his insights. I was eager to return and deepen my friendship with the family. 'Come back whenever you want to,' he said, as if reading my mind, before I clambered on to my donkey and steered a hopeful course home.

A few weeks later I returned to find Muglid under his usual tree with a small crowd of people around him. 'Don't worry. You aren't intruding,' he said, after I expressed my concern that I might be interrupting his meeting.

One of his visitors was lying on the ground in obvious discomfort. Muglid instructed his son to bring up one of his donkeys. A few minutes later, with help from the onlookers, the man was lifted on to its back. The donkey had no saddle and his rider was not going anywhere either. Muglid took a short length of rope and despite his groans proceeded to tie the man's legs together under the stomach of the animal.

Clearly thirsty the donkey drank several buckets of water in quick succession. A few minutes later its stomach began to push outwards and as it did so the man on top of it began to cry out in pain.

'What is going on?' I asked.

'Just be patient,' Muglid said.

There was the noise of a click a few minutes later, a look of relief on the face of the man, and when his legs were untied he was able to dismount on his own. Without the previous assistance he had needed, he began to hobble around to considerable applause from the spectators.

'It's a technique I learned from my father,' Muglid explained after his guests departed. A few days previously one of his neighbours had fallen from a tree and dislocated his hip. His family had brought him to Muglid, who as well as being a teacher and farmer was a well known traditional healer in the district. 'Bring him back the day after tomorrow,' he had instructed. One of his donkeys was then deprived of water for several days until it became desperate. When the buckets were placed in front of it the water was consumed in a few feverish gulps. The rest I had seen.

'The stomach expands in exactly the way that is needed to push the dislocated bone back into its socket. It may be painful and uncomfortable but it works,' Muglid concluded, 'just like my wooden wheel.'

I was impressed but wondered why the patient had not gone to one of the clinics in town, or the local hospital where several doctors advertised their services. Muglid laughed. 'Sometimes I have people coming here who have been sent to me by these same doctors.'

Traditional medicine had been in Muglid's family for several generations, he explained. He had learned about herbs and their medicinal properties from his mother. His father had been a well-known bonesetter in the area, famous for treating complicated fractures.

'How do you manage without X-rays, without injections, without anything?' I asked.

'Through experience. That's what all medicine is about and you don't have to go to college for five years to learn it either. Don't look so surprised,' he said, noticing my astonishment. 'What do you think we did before we had professional doctors?'

Muglid went on to tell me that there were two types of traditional healer in the community. The first, like him, treated physical ailments such as broken bones, stomach aches, minor infections and fever. Although there was no formal system of registration they either learned their skills from other family members or served an apprenticeship with a recognized practitioner. Only when they were deemed to have enough experience would they be allowed to practise on their own. If their remedies failed to work then people would simply vote with their feet and go elsewhere.

The other group of healers, called 'Faqis', were more religious. They would make amulets and charms, write prayers on pieces of paper which when dissolved in water were said to cure a variety of ailments. There was something of an ambivalent attitude towards them in the community, claimed Muglid. While people respected them for what they could do, they feared them at the same time.

'These healers are believed to derive their powers from spirits, called Jinn, and some of these are good and others bad. The evil spirits give them powers that can be used to cause harm to others, as well as giving them the ability to heal.'

Many of them, Muglid continued, were itinerant. They travelled the country with little more than the clothes on their backs and their potions and charms. Sheltered and fed by people in the towns and villages they passed through, they were reputed to bring good fortune to any household that looked after them.

'The more orthodox Muslims in the community believe them to be little more than fakes,' Muglid continued. 'They say these people exploit the superstition and ignorance of others, but most people see them as genuine holy men who deserve respect.'

'Does their medicine work?' I asked. 'Can they do what they say?'

Muglid paused for a moment before continuing. 'As a healer I know that a large part of what I do arises from the belief by the patient that I can help him. It's the same with these Faqis. Able to capture and exploit this belief they can work wonders.'

As Muglid spoke I began to realize how ignorant I was not just about Islam, the predominant religion in the country, but the cultural practices that influenced and informed it. Like Christianity, Islam had its rules and regulations. I knew that Muslims had to pray five times a day, fast during Ramadan, make the occasional pilgrimage to Mecca to honour their prophet, and practise charity and good works. But when Muglid began to talk about 'saints' and 'religious healers', and the fear and reverence people displayed towards them, I realised there was more to this religion than the outward show I was familiar with.

Even the geography of the area, the physical landscape, was informed by people's beliefs Muglid continued. 'On the way to my home did you pass a tree on the side of the road with lots of ribbons?' he asked.

I had, thinking that some cloth had caught in the branches

or that children had decided to decorate it to pass their time.

'These ribbons are a sign of respect to honour the spirit that lives in that location. Some women go there in the hope that it will improve their chances of becoming pregnant.'

He pointed to a house nearby and the gates and walls which had been elaborately painted. Again I had thought that this was nothing more than an attempt by some family to brighten up their surroundings. Muglid explained that the patterns and signs had more than just a decorative significance. They were designed to protect the house and its occupants from evil spirits or the jealousy of neighbours. It was the same with much of the personal ornamentation people wore. They were not only there to display wealth or enhance someone's beauty, but to protect their wearers from harm and misfortune.

Noticing my curiosity Muglid asked me what I was doing the following week.

'Nothing,' I replied. 'Do you have anything in mind?'

'Come back next Friday and I'll take you to a place that you will find interesting.'

The following Friday a car was waiting with Muglid and his excited children. His wife was there too with some of her sisters. I counted fifteen passengers crammed into the pickup with myself as number sixteen.

Instead of heading north or south along the river as I had expected the vehicle turned towards the desert. It was a long, bumpy ride of over an hour. Several times Muglid had to catch me to prevent me falling off.

'This is what I wanted to show you,' he said, as we approached a small clump of trees that emerged from the dunes. Hidden within them and overlooking a small spring that bubbled from the ground was a hut covered in white plaster. Numerous bottles had been stuck into the sand around it.

It was the tomb of one of the local saints and we were not the only ones there. Several vehicles were parked around, their occupants sitting among the dunes. The bottles in the sand, Muglid explained, had pieces of paper inside them. These were the prayers that people left behind. According to Muglid there were numerous such tombs scattered around the Sahara; places of pilgrimage that people visited to seek relief from illness, or wealth if they had fallen on hard times, or a child if a woman was infertile. Some of the more famous saints had special celebratory days and people from miles around, some from as far away as Egypt and Morocco, would visit on that particular date.

During the picnic that the family brought with them, Muglid's wife and her sisters disappeared in the direction of the tomb, only the girls allowed to go with them. They returned laughing and giggling and told Muglid to mind his own business when he enquired what they had been up to. I was struck, not only by the importance of this visit to the family, the obvious respect they had for the place as they brushed away the sand that had collected on one side of the tomb, but by the light-hearted enjoyment that accompanied it as well. It made me realize how little I understood about a religion and culture noted for its formality and austerity.

I was struck again by how little I really knew of the lives of the people around me and wondered what I would need to do, what other doors would have to open, to say with conviction I had penetrated this society. Maybe I would always be an outsider looking in, prevented by culture, tradition and history from anything more than superficial insights.

As usual, Muglid was calm and reassuring. 'You cannot expect people to disclose themselves until they get to know you first, to see that you respect them,' he said as we jolted our way back in the late afternoon towards Dongola in the distance.

'I don't know if I should let you see this,' Muglid said a few weeks later during another visit to his home. 'Since you're our friend and since you're curious about how we live here in Dongola, my wife has given her permission.'

He steered me towards the inside of the house and the large room reserved for guests and visitors. It was occupied this time by a crowd of women, their noise and chatter in sharp contrast to the demure and whispered conversations they normally conducted in the presence of men.

Muglid, usually deferred to by the women of his household, was this time brusquely ushered by his wife to a corner of the room, while I followed sheepishly behind. It was made clear that we were to do nothing more than watch, that we were to be as quiet as mice and that our presence was being tolerated rather than welcomed.

'Is it a wedding ceremony?' I whispered to Muglid, when some women in the centre of a space that had been cleared around them began to beat some drums.

'Just wait and see,' Muglid counselled, urging patience.

Up till then I had thought we were the only males present but another man appeared from one of the nearby rooms a short while later. Tall, bearded, dressed in traditional garb and waving a stick above his head, the loud burst of applause that greeted his entry made me wonder even more why Muglid and I appeared to be so unwelcome. 'Who is he?' I asked.

'It's not a he,' Muglid replied. 'Look closely.'

I had thought there was something strange about the man's appearance, something not quite right in the way he danced, in the movements he made. It was only when the beard fell away, however, revealing the face of a young woman that I realized how mistaken I had been.

As the women giggled and laughed, the beard was put back in place and the 'man' continued his provocative dance among them. I was even more surprised a short while later when he pulled a cigar from his pocket, lit it up and began to smoke to even wilder applause and the obvious amusement of everyone present. A bottle then appeared which was passed around. From the reactions of the women who took some swigs, I suspected it did not contain water either.

As the drumming quickened and the women began to dance too, in a way that I would never have expected in this normally reserved community, Muglid's wife approached us to say it was time for us to leave. We had seen enough, she said, and the women were uncomfortable with us watching the rest of the proceedings. Muglid raised no objections as we exited the room, the party behind us clearly moving up another gear.

Outside, in the shade of his usual tree, Muglid explained

that we had seen part of a 'Zar' ceremony. Practised exclusively by women it was a mixture of religious ritual and a kind
of collective emotional release. I remarked that I had not seen
much resembling religion in what I had witnessed, but he
pointed out that the dancing that took place, which would
continue all day, was heavily influenced by Sufi traditions. The
ecstatic nature of the ceremony was similar to the trances
incurred by the religious orders he had talked about during my
previous visit.

Where the Zar came from, what its origins were, how it had
arrived in their community he could not say. He did know that
it had been part of their traditions for some time, since he
could remember being ushered out of the house as a boy when
his mother had once hosted a ceremony.

The Zar was invoked for different reasons, he continued.
This one had been for the benefit of the young woman who
had dressed up as a man. She was a neighbour whose marriage
was in difficulty because she could not fall pregnant. Since
they could find no physical reason for her inability to conceive,
it was assumed she had been influenced by some discontented
spirit. The purpose of the ceremony was to allow her to
become possessed so that this spirit could then state its
demands. This could be a set of new clothes, a pair of shoes,
her husband's agreement to some previously failed request.
Once appeased, it would leave her alone so that she could fall
pregnant.

'There are men who oppose it,' he replied to my question.
'But some of us accept that women need a space of their own, a
time where they can express themselves without their normal
inhibitions.' He went on to say that despite the appearance of
an event where things got out of hand, the ceremony had rules
and regulations. The meetings were always presided over by a
Sheikha, who instructed everyone on how to behave. The
drinking and smoking I had seen were ritualistic and flirta-
tious, a means of caricaturing the behaviour of men, and not
an opportunity for the women to get drunk.

As we listened to the noise and drumming that came from
Muglid's home I remarked again that there was much more I

had to learn about his society. Many things continued to baffle me and the longer I stayed the more confused and impenetrable it seemed.

'Never mind,' said Muglid, as he proceeded to pour the tea that had suddenly appeared from the house, reassuring us that we had not been entirely forgotten. 'I have lived here all my life and there are still things I know nothing about.'

5

Slow boat to Ed Debba

Several months into the start of the school year the headmaster called us out of our classes. We had attended meetings before: to discuss extracurricular activities for the girls, forthcoming exams and events planned to raise funds for the school. This one seemed more urgent since we were told to suspend what we were doing and come immediately. In his hand was a letter from the provincial education office, just delivered to him, and which he had been instructed to share.

'Due to the impossibility of finding a solution to the strike by teachers in Khartoum and neighbouring towns, the Ministry of Education announces an immediate closure of all schools for an indefinite period.'

'Did you know there was a strike?' I whispered to Abdel Majid, who like the other teachers manifested no expression of shock or astonishment.

'No,' he replied, shrugging his shoulders, 'but since there are strikes nearly every year it's hardly surprising.'

'Every year! What for?'

'Teachers want more money and the Government says it hasn't got any. There is a strike for a few weeks. Then the Government finds some money, the teachers compromise and everyone goes back to work.'

I remembered the confusion that surrounded the start of school term, and the impossibility of getting information from the officials who were supposed to be running the system.

'What are we supposed to do during this time? Sit around and wait for an announcement?'

Abdel Majid looked at me like a teacher confronting one of

his more obstinate pupils. 'Sudan is a big country,' he replied. 'You say you want to travel – now's your chance.'

'How do I find out when this thing is over?'

'Ask if schools are open. If they're closed you can continue to the next town.'

By the time I got home John had already packed his bags. 'I'm going back to Khartoum so I can remember what a white, porcelain toilet feels like,' he said. 'See you in a few weeks.'

Arthur had decided to stay, to catch up on writing his book. 'What will you do?' he asked.

Taking Abdel Majid's advice I decided to travel – and what better place than the province to which I had been posted.

'But don't you want to go somewhere else?' he asked.

'No' I replied, reminding him that our province was bigger than Scotland and that all I had seen was Dongola and the surrounding villages.

If you want to move from one part of Sudan to another in comfort and style you take a plane but, as I had already discovered, the service was not only costly but unreliable.

If you were determined to get to wherever you were going you took a bus, but then you needed to be prepared for an uncomfortable few days: extreme heat; dust in your eyes, ears and nostrils; jolting over rough terrain, wondering whether the track was leading you to the next village or the middle of the desert where you would never be found again.

'There is an alternative,' Abdel Majid informed me. 'If you want to see our country from a different perspective you can take the Nile steamer.'

I looked up 'Nile steamer' in the guidebook that had become our bible. The ferry from Dongola, it read, sometimes experienced long delays and had a high probability of getting stuck in the sands that shifted around the river.

'If you want to get where you are going in a hurry,' it advised, 'don't take the Nile steamer.'

Time seemed not to be a problem. 'It's unlikely this strike will be over in less than a month,' was Abdel Majid's best guess. 'I wouldn't worry about getting stuck.'

The ferry ran between Dongola and a small town called Karima, several hundred kilometres to the south, and beyond that were the Nile Rapids, a series of awkward rocks that made progress further upstream impossible. I was unable to find out from the guidebook or anyone I spoke to, the history or logic of the service, apart from the fact that it seemed a more comfortable way of moving along the river.

At the small, wooden kiosk where I purchased my ticket an old, grizzled supervisor asked which 'class' I wanted.

'Class?'

'Yes. First class, Second class, or Ordinary.'

Things were looking up.

'What will I get for First class and how much will it cost?'

'Your own cabin. Tea or coffee in the morning. No mosquitoes. And it's only double the price of Second Class.'

Definitely worth the extra money I thought, and purchased a first class ticket, a series of vouchers for dinner, and a timetable which said that the ferry would depart at 2.30 the following afternoon. 'Passengers who are late,' it said in the small print, 'will be left behind.'

As it turned out, the Nile steamer left four days later than the date stamped on my ticket. Every morning, afternoon and evening I would march down to the harbour to find out if it had arrived. 'Bukra Inshallah,' was the inevitable reply. By the morning of the third day I wondered whether it actually existed and began to enquire about the bus. Arrive it eventually did, later that afternoon, announcing itself with a loud blast of its horn that brought a crowd of people rushing to the pier, myself along with them.

As it rounded a bend in the river, still some distance away, it seemed much grander than I had expected. Then I realized when it got nearer that it was not just one boat but three tied together. Against the currents that pulled and pushed it in all directions it seemed impossible to navigate. Would it be safe? Would it sink? Would my journey down the Nile be as bumpy as the bus I had been determined to avoid? The passengers as they disembarked, however, seemed none the worse for wear. No one threw themselves on the ground or hugged their relatives in relief. The only complaint I heard was that it had been delayed in some village because of lack of fuel. With time on my hands I decided to proceed.

'Come back tomorrow,' was the reply I received when the crowd dispersed and I presented my ticket. The ferry needed to load up on supplies and had to take coal on board for the engines. Nor was it safe to travel at night. It would depart the following day at the appointed time, 'Inshallah'.

Abdullah, the steward, took my ticket and bags when I arrived the next day.

'This way please,' he said and took me to a cabin besides the captain's quarters and the bridge that he said I could visit whenever I wanted. He was here to look after the first class passengers. If I needed anything I was to call him at any time.

He looked a sprightly forty year old but told me he was almost sixty. Hard work kept him young, he boasted. His English was good but every few sentences were punctuated with expletives.

'Scottish people taught me English,' he enthused after I had told him where I came from. He had been in the merchant navy for some twenty years. He had sailed all over the Indian Ocean and the Pacific. There were lots of Sudanese seamen who were cooks and stewards on big ships, he said. Their polite manners were well known and appreciated by captains all over the world.

'We are much more popular than the fucking Somalis,' he added.

The cabins reserved for the first class passengers were located on the principal ferry. This was an old steamer with a large, smoky funnel in the centre of the ship and a paddle at the end that propelled the whole edifice through the water. The engines were made in Glasgow, a fact that was announced on a metal plaque in the centre of the ship as if to reassure everyone of their reliability.

Fastened by steel wires on the left side was a boat with the second class cabins and on the other side an open topped barge that was reserved for the 'ordinary' passengers. This was where most people had gathered, competing for the limited space with goats, donkeys and a large pile of coal. It resembled a market. People set up various stalls, surrounding themselves with goods and possessions, engaging in conversation with their neighbours. I realized then that the ferry was not just a means of transport down the river but functioned as a kind of floating village as well. I had wondered why it took some five days to travel the distance between Dongola and Karima further south. Now I had my answer.

The slow, languid river I had contemplated from the banks of Dongola belied a more unpredictable and powerful current. When our ferry swung out from its mooring I could feel it surge around us. This was another reason the journey took so long, I discovered, since we had to push against the river the entire route. The return journey, by comparison, was much quicker, Abdullah explained, sometimes taking less than three days.

As the funnel belched a cloud of black smoke and our single paddle turned, we began to inch forward. A thick wave splashed the deck in front of us as the river resisted. A few hours later we had not yet progressed beyond the point where my donkey had taken me on a previous occasion.

Abdel Majid was right. The country we passed through was very different. It seemed much more lush and fertile for a start, and less threatened by the desert that only occasionally intruded from behind the screen of trees lining its banks. The dependence of the Nile communities on the water and soil it provided was also evident. The river rose when the rains fell further south and the land was regularly flooded for several weeks, sometimes longer if it was a good season. When it returned to its normal level there was a thick layer of mud left behind that provided the basis of the country's agriculture.

'If it wasn't for Ethiopia there wouldn't be a northern Sudan,' was an observation I remembered, referring to the fact that most of the soil carried by the river came from the Highlands of Ethiopia, thousands of kilometres away.

The two countries had almost gone to war when Ethiopia

announced one year that it planned to build a dam on the lower Nile that would significantly decrease the flow of water downstream. Egypt had swayed into the argument too, claiming it would blow up any structure that would reduce the supply on which it was so completely dependent.

'The wars of the future will be fought over water,' the article went on to claim, pointing out that tensions and conflicts in the Middle East and North Africa were not just about oil.

Sometime later, having retired to my cramped cabin to take some rest, there was a knocking on the door. 'The captain has decided to see you now,' Abdullah announced, as if I had previously requested an audience. 'On the Bridge.'

The other passengers had been summoned too, but the captain was easy to pick out. He was dressed in a crisp white uniform, with a cap on his head and an obvious air of authority. It was as if the ship he was commanding was a grand ocean liner and not a ramshackle collection of wooden boats tied together and barely managing to struggle up the Nile.

'Bridge' was a misnomer too. Apart from the steering wheel, a pipe with a funnel to shout instructions down and one large window, it was nothing more than an extension of the captain's living quarters. There was a mattress on the floor, a wardrobe, a table with chairs and a small alcove from which Abdullah produced cups of tea and coffee for the assembled guests. A cat eyed us suspiciously from one of the corners.

With his cap removed the captain looked familiar, bearing an uncanny resemblance to the headmaster of my school. 'You must be the English teacher in Dongola,' he said, when I was ushered in front of him to shake hands. 'My brother has told me all about you.'

Despite his airs and graces he was talkative and forthcoming. He had served in the merchant navy for many years but at several levels above Abdullah and without acquiring any of his colourful language. He had been the captain of several vessels sailing around the continent, had studied for a year in Southampton and once visited Scotland where he remembered the whisky and 'the beautiful girls' from Glasgow whose speech he could never understand. He had finally returned to captain 'this small ferry on the Nile,' a position he added, with some candour, that was only a step away from retirement.

'Sailing down this river,' he continued, 'is nothing like as hazardous or exciting as some of my previous adventures.' The Pacific storms he had encountered had been much more exciting, he added, and I thought a tidal wave rushing up the river would have pleased him immensely. But even a placid journey up the Nile had its moments. On one occasion, he recalled with enthusiasm, the barges had swung loose and had pulled them perilously close to rocks that would have sunk them. They managed to cut the wires at the last minute and nothing worse had happened than a few donkeys fallen overboard and some shaken up passengers. 'That's not likely to happen again' he said wistfully.

Our group on the bridge consisted of a number of merchants from Dongola, a few teachers from the province, a cousin of the captain and another European. The latter manifested little enthusiasm when I went over to introduce myself. As it turned out, Stanley came from Doncaster and was a train enthusiast. He had travelled thousands of miles for the privilege of sitting in a train made in his home town many years previously and recording the details in a little book. He had little sense of humour and seemed irritated when I asked him whether a boat whose engines were made in Glasgow could be classified as something connected to his home country.

He did become effusive, however, when I asked him about trains, since I was interested in doing the next leg of my journey in one of them. The train from Khartoum to Wadi Halfa in the north of the province was pulled by an old steam engine manufactured in England in the 1940s. He went on to inform me about the amount of coal it needed in a day and the number of carriages it could pull behind it.

In his book of dates and numbers there were several photos he had taken of his travels in Africa, India and other parts of the world that had lots of railways. There were no photos of the native people he must have met, unless, of course, they happened to be driving the train that was his real interest. When I asked what he thought about the Sudanese people he had met on his journey from Khartoum, the families he must have met, the friends that were so easily made, it was as if I had asked him about some exotic species that only existed on the periphery of his vision.

As we left the bridge, Hassan informed me that the captain had invited me for supper. It turned out I was the only guest.

'English people are a strange mix,' he replied, when I asked him how he had enjoyed his time in England. People in general had been polite and hospitable, he said, and had not shown any animosity towards him, but behind their good manners there was kind of frostiness that had been difficult to penetrate, a point beyond which he would not be welcome. One of his adventures had taken place in Southampton, where he had made the mistake of dating a girl from town. He had been threatened by members of her family who told him that a black man from Africa would not be welcome in their household.

The extent of racism had varied in different places, he was keen to point out, and cities like Manchester, Newcastle and Glasgow had been different; warmer and friendlier than London.

What had surprised him most was 'a deep ignorance' of Africa. Many people were unaware where Sudan was, or the size of the continent to which it belonged, the history, the different religions. Their lack of curiosity had intrigued him. When he introduced himself and mentioned where he was from there had been little or no attempt to find out more.

'Why did this surprise you?' I asked, remembering my own ignorance about Africa.

'When I was young some of the teachers in my school came from England,' he replied. 'I remember how they pushed us, how they said that without education we would never get ahead. One of our best lecturers at college came from Scotland. I had the impression that everyone there must be educated and curious and eager to find out about other places.' Yet curiosity about strangers was something he had not encountered in the time he had been there.

'It is different here,' he said. 'Even a simple villager will take time for strangers, will be curious as to who they are, where they are from, what they think about Sudan and our culture. Isn't this something you have noticed,' he continued, 'the people who want to know your business and how you do things where you come from?'

I agreed, remembering the numerous discussions with strangers in Dongola, their questions that at times had seemed like an interrogation, everyone eager to find out who I was, where I was from and yes, what I thought about them and their country.

Despite the information I had first received, the ferry did move at night. Against the current that continued to resist us, however, our progress seemed so slow that if we had bumped into anything I doubt whether it would have harmed us. The sandbanks were the things to worry about, the captain said, since even at our pace it was possible to get stuck on one of them for several days. They had once been stranded for almost a week and only when they had conveyed all the passengers to the shore and thrown their supply of coal overboard had they been able to float free.

As we spoke, the captain clicked on a switch beside him. This lit an array of lights around the ferry so that now, more than ever, we resembled a floating village. Darkness was pushed aside and the river ahead of us illuminated, a bank lined with trees and a group of camels that ran off when the light hit them. To make sure we didn't run aground someone had been posted to the bow of the ship. The captain pointed him out, presiding over a large drum that he was to bang whenever a hazard presented itself.

While these lights kept us safe and relatively sure of our progress upstream, they also attracted every sort and variety of flying insect from miles around. There was a permanent cloud of moths, beetles and other bugs around the ship with bats swooping in and out to consume them.

The absence of mosquitoes in the first class cabins turned out to be a claim that was only partly true. Earlier that evening Abdullah had appeared with a spray which he had used in our cabins to exterminate them, but with no screens on the doors or windows, the only way to keep them out was by sealing yourself in. It was still summer and the stifling heat meant a choice between suffocation and the risk of malaria. In the end, I opted to open the windows having previously covered myself in a smelly chemical that Stanley had had the foresight to bring with him and had been willing to share.

My first thought when I woke was that we had run aground on one of the sandbanks. There was no forward movement and the engines had stopped. I expected to see a crowd of agitated passengers arguing with the crew, throwing their animals and goods overboard to lighten our load. I added another few days in my head to the five scheduled to complete the journey and hoped that the predictions about the strike were true and that I would not be stranded in the middle of the river while the girls waited for their English lessons.

When I stumbled through the door I could see that we had halted beside a small town, that passengers were disembarking and others getting on and that our lack of movement was in fact deliberate. On time and as previously announced, Abdullah delivered a cup of tea and the news that we had reached the town of Ed Debba, one of the settlements between Dongola and Karima.

'How long will we be here?' I asked.

'We will have to take on more fuel,' he answered. At various places along the river, Ed Debba included, some time would be needed to locate supplies and agree a price. There was a weekly market too, that some of the merchants from Dongola wanted to attend. Most importantly the captain had a cousin whom he wanted to visit. It would all depend on when he concluded his business. But Ed Debba was worth a look, Abdullah claimed. 'You have a few hours, maybe more.'

'How will I know when it is time to leave?' I asked.

'You'll hear a loud blast of the horn and then you have five minutes to get on board. Try not to worry!'

Like Dongola, Ed Debba spread itself along the river so that where it started and ended was difficult to say. Worried that the captain might conclude his visit earlier than expected I did not venture far. The market was not as big and grand as the one I was used to but had the same noise, chatter and excitement. Maybe because of the large number of camels that crowded its narrow streets and the sand dunes that swept up to the edge of its houses the town seemed more of a desert settlement than the communities I was familiar with. I ended up drinking coffee, from a place where I could watch the people going about their business while keeping an eye on the ferry.

I had been used in Dongola to people coming up to shake my hand, to find out where I was from, to buy me a coffee as an introduction to the questions they were eager to ask. It did not surprise me, therefore, when one of the residents of the town did the same. Dressed in a native Jellabiya and a white scarf around his head the man who sat down at my table looked every bit an established member of the community, so it turned out a surprise when Robert announced that he was a teacher like myself and had been there for over a year. He spoke fluent Arabic and seemed popular too, judging by the people who came up to greet him and ask him how he was.

Unlike myself, Arthur or John, he had raised his hand the previous year when he was asked where he wanted to be posted. The reason he had chosen a small, isolated settlement on the edge of the desert was that it gave him an opportunity to interact with the people he was curious about, the nomads of the eastern Sahara. Although they were not resident in Ed Debba itself, they came there frequently to sell their camels and goats and purchase provisions. Robert's intention was to find out what he could about them, become 'accepted' in their society and undertake some of the journeys they still made across the desert with their animals.

'Why?' I asked. 'What's your motivation?'

He shrugged his shoulders, mentioning a book he had once

read about nomads and the film *Lawrence of Arabia*. 'No better or worse a reason than that of anyone else here. What was yours?' As I stumbled through my answer I was conscious again of how much my own decision lacked the purpose I had seen in others, that I still had to figure out why I was here.

'Come and see the animal I bought last week,' he said, changing the subject. 'He's in the camel park.'

In one of the squares behind the central market a space had been reserved for what seemed to be the entire camel population of northern Sudan. Stately, indifferent and poised when alone, in company the camels became quarrelsome, temperamental beasts who constantly snarled at each other, slavered over members of the opposite sex and stank horribly. A few boys had been employed to keep order and this was done by whacking them across their rumps with a heavy wooden stick whenever they misbehaved.

Robert's camel was a large, white brute who was clearly in a foul mood. He seemed uninterested when we approached him, showed no sign of recognizing his new master and had cleared a considerable space around himself by snapping at the other animals until they had backed off. They seemed as intimidated as I was.

'Why have you bought the most difficult animal in the country?' I asked.

He confessed he was not sure if he had made the right choice. The previous week he had asked one of his friends 'who knows about these things' to help him buy a camel. Robert had felt it was unlikely he would be able to mix with nomadic society if he didn't have one. 'How can you join a motorbike gang if you haven't got a machine?' was how he put it.

Robert's friend had picked this one out immediately, but the men they bought him from seemed reluctant to sell. 'That is a good sign,' his friend had told him.

They said he was temperamental, when Robert insisted this was the one he wanted. One of them displayed a scar on his leg where the animal had bitten him. It didn't like being ridden they told him. It took two of them, one holding down the ring on the end of his nose, to get a saddle on its back.

Yet as a crowd gathered round to witness this strange transaction – a white man buying a camel – it was clear that this was one of the finest animals on display. As it turned out, the principal reason they didn't want to sell their camel was because of its 'popularity.' In other words they preferred to put it out to stud. When Robert's friend finally named the price they had hoped for they shook hands and agreed.

As it spat and hissed in our direction I had doubts as to whether Robert, who confessed to never having ridden a camel before coming to Sudan, would be able to control him. But as obstinate and difficult as the animal was, there was something just as hard and obstinate about Robert. It was difficult to pin down exactly. I had only known him for a short while, but he communicated an attitude of fixed determination, a commitment to see his Sudanese ambitions fully realized. Maybe he would win this battle after all.

As we finished another coffee, Robert pointed to a group of men who were clearly different from the people around them. It was not just the clothes they wore, or their swagger as they walked around the various stalls inspecting the goods, or the heavy swords that some of them held across their shoulders. The space around them reminded me of the space around Robert's camel, the territory that had been marked out which warned others not to intrude.

This was a group of nomads Robert had befriended. The previous week he had asked them whether he could ride with them. 'In a few months time,' they had replied. That was when they would be ready to move to their winter pastures. There was another condition too, Robert said. They had told him he would have to convert, that they were not prepared to travel with someone who was not a Muslim.

'So what will you do?' I asked, curious as to whether his principles would outweigh his ambitions.

'I've already decided to do so,' he replied, mentioning that he had recently announced in the local mosque his intention to become a Muslim. I said nothing, but he seemed slightly defensive, as if he felt a need to justify his decision.

'There isn't that much difference between Islam and Christianity,' he continued. 'By and large we have the same prophets, adhere to the same principles, and worship the same god. Besides, the nomads I've already hung out with don't seem to take it very seriously either. In the few days I spent with them in their camp I rarely saw them pray.'

'It's more a social issue,' he continued, when I asked him why they insisted he convert if they did not take their religion 'that seriously'.

'If you have a small group that is bound so tightly together in such a hostile environment you don't want divisions or a sense that someone doesn't belong. I don't believe it's my soul they are worried about but their own sense of cohesion. Perhaps they also want to see how serious I am about keeping their company.'

'Will you have to get circumcised too?' I asked, wondering how far Robert was prepared to go.

'No one has said I have to,' he replied firmly. 'If anyone does I'll tell them that religion has nothing to do with my private parts.'

It was clear from the raised voices and the arguments we witnessed that there was little affection between the townspeople and the nomads. This was typical across the Sahara, Robert explained, and in Mali and Mauritania had escalated into a full scale civil war that had lasted for several decades. In Sudan there were frequent conflicts. There was fighting in Chad, Ethiopia and Niger. 'Governments resent these people travelling across their borders, with smuggled goods and no papers. Nomads resent the controls on their traditional freedom to go wherever they want. Lines on a map have never been of consequence to them.'

In recent years this legacy of historical conflict had worsened. Much of the current fighting, Robert explained, was over territory, especially in the wake of the discovery of oil and minerals which had transformed previously unvalued desert into a commodity to be fought over. 'If it wasn't for the fact that the merchants in this town need goats and camels and the nomads need sugar, tea and other goods both would prefer to have nothing to do with each other.'

His own interest in their society was also frowned upon. There was genuine confusion among his friends in town and fellow teachers. 'They are dirty and unclean. They are thieves and liars,' one of his colleagues had warned.

Such arguments had not fazed him. They were similar to the kinds of attitudes and behaviour displayed towards travellers and gypsies in other societies, he said. 'What is curious is that not so long ago this was the predominant way of life for many people in this part of the world. Maybe they are disliked because they remind all of us where we once came from.'

As Robert spoke I wondered if part of his interest in their society was tinged with a certain amount of exoticism. He had been disappointed by what he had found in the town of Ed Debba, he had said. When I pressed him as to what he meant he replied that it was too similar to the society he had left behind in England.

The rather dismissive attitude he displayed towards the people he now lived among, the townspeople who had obviously embraced him, surprised me. If what he said about the predominant attitudes towards nomadic society was true then clearly it was reprehensible, but I felt there was an element of that same attitude in his own manner of talking about the settled people of the province, who had somehow failed to live up to his expectations. Was their desire for televisions, cars, radios, fridges and development so reprehensible? Was the fact that they had the same ambitions as people in our own society so disappointing? Perhaps Robert's interest in discovering a society not yet tainted by these aspirations said more about him and what he was escaping from, than the people he seemed so determined to find.

I had no time to establish the answers to my questions. As the blast of the horn signalled the imminent departure of the ferry I felt they would probably have been unwelcome too. We had only just met. Single minded and determined, Robert might not appreciate such observations. No doubt his own journey would either modify or confirm the prejudices he had brought with him. We all have our journeys to make and no one can travel for us.

We shook hands and I wished him the best. I had enjoyed meeting a fellow teacher who displayed such a keen interest in the country. His enthusiasm and drive were infectious and made me more determined to pursue my own travels and be open to the experiences they would bring. 'Good luck,' I said, telling him I hoped we would meet again after his journey so that he could tell me about what he had found and the people he had finally discovered.

6

From Kadima to Wadi Halfa

Over the few weeks I had been in Sudan there had been little discussion about politics either with my colleagues at school or the friends I had made in Dongola. I could see that the President was not popular but conversations about him were normally abrupt, short and cautious. 'There are too many people listening,' Abdel Majid once confided when I asked him about Nimeiri and why he was so rarely discussed in public.

His photo was everywhere, frowning at us from the head-master's office in school and from the walls of the Government Ministries in town. His picture was framed in the captain's cabin. Failure to put it up in public places was regarded not as a careless omission but a deliberate act of political subversion, Abdel Majid had told me.

He was even depicted on the Sudanese currency, something of a novelty on the continent where presidents usually had to wait until they died or left office before receiving that honour.

'But it was not a smart move to put his face on our money,' I was told by one of the teachers on the ferry as we stood one day at the stern of the boat. Ismail taught in the boy's secondary school in Dongola. I had met him a few times before but he was more Arthur and John's friend than mine. Taking advantage of the strike at school, something he endorsed as one of the union representatives in town, he was visiting his family in Kurti, a few days downriver from Dongola.

'Why was it not smart?'

'Because it gives people a chance to show their dissent without being caught. Haven't you noticed that all our bank notes have been defaced?' he said, pulling a wad of them from his pocket. On all of them the President's eyes had been pricked out, two neat little holes that I had never noticed before.

'It's pathetic, isn't it?' he continued, with some candour. 'We've reached a stage where people's opposition to the President can only be expressed by sabotaging our own currency.'

The Sudanese, he continued, had no great expectations of their political leaders, but when Nimeiri had come to power there had been considerable excitement in many parts of the country. He had promised and delivered an end to the civil war between the north and south, embraced a kind of left wing, socialist agenda and promised a new era of Sudanese politics without the patronage and corruption of the past. Big schemes, faster development, religious tolerance, acceptance of cultural diversity were the slogans that had won him considerable popular support in the early years of his rule.

'Naïve of us to have listened,' the teacher continued, listing the corruption, the political favours, the rise of Islamic militancy, the increasing intransigence of the military and police that now characterized his regime.

The political opposition was centred on a figure called Siddiq el Mahdi. His great grandfather was the famous Mahdi who had killed General Gordon in Khartoum and created an Islamic republic in the previous century. I remembered Laurence Olivier dressed up in native gear and Charlton Heston having his head chopped off and stuck on a pole while the Sudanese celebrated. I also remembered the poem by Rudyard Kipling about the famous warriors with elaborate hair styles who had fought for the Mahdi against the British and inflicted one of the few defeats they had ever suffered:

So ere's to you, Fuzzy Wuzzy, at your 'ome in the Soudan
You're a pore benighted 'eathen but a first class fightin' man
An ere's to you, Fuzzy Wuzzy, with your 'ayrick 'ead of 'air
You big black boundin' beggar – for you broke a British square!

Ismail was scathing about the Mahdi's great grandson too, claiming he was part of the clique which had had its chance after independence to improve the country and spectacularly failed. 'This is our problem,' he said with considerable passion. 'We believe that because someone happens to be the grandson of a famous historical figure, if we hand over all responsibility they will somehow solve our problems. Soon enough our politicians and leaders end up believing what we tell them, that they can do nothing wrong.'

Too much trust was at the heart of many of the contemporary problems that affected the continent, Ismail went on to say. He was a communist, had been arrested several times for his political activities and was concerned that I seemed to have no firm political beliefs myself. 'I am travelling without any baggage,' was construed by him as a lamentable lack of any convictions on my part.

He handed me a book when we arrived at his village a few hours later. It was a treatise by Karl Marx, which I had once studied as part of the philosophy degree I had abandoned before coming to his country.

'I'll read it,' I said, as he exited the ferry, knowing full well that it would be packed away with the other text books that had remained unopened since I had arrived.

Four days after we left Dongola, Abdullah knocked on my door to tell me we were approaching Karima and would be there within the hour. I had to ask him several times if he was sure, since it was one of the few occasions when an original forecast about departure or arrival would have turned out to be correct.

'We said four days. Didn't you believe us?'

By that stage my cabin on the ferry, the bridge where I regularly dined with the captain, the barge where the ordinary class passengers were always welcoming had begun to feel like home. Occasionally that bubble of familiarity had been exchanged for a brief sojourn in one of the small towns along the way. I had enjoyed moving in and out of different locations, encountering people who were always willing to converse and who were not timid about their curiosity. After a few hours, sometimes longer if the captain happened to have a relative to visit, I was always pleased to return to our floating village and the group of people travelling with me.

'So what will you do now?' the captain asked, as we shook hands for the last time.

'Go to the nearest school to find out what is happening,' I replied. 'If the strike is over, I don't want your brother to get upset that I'm not working.'

Although Karima was a sizeable town it only took me a few minutes to locate a school a short distance from where we had disembarked. There were closed gates, no signs of any pupils, and a bored guard who shrugged his shoulders and said he had no idea when classes would resume. An official I met at the nearby education office could also shed no light as to when the strike might be over.

'Continue your journey,' was his advice when I asked him what he thought I should do. 'Even if they come to an agreement tomorrow it will be about a week before everyone gets back to work.'

The train station in Karima was of another time and place. If you ignored the sight of the desert stretching behind it, the large crowd of men in jellabiyas milling around and its cracked and blistered paintwork it might have been manufactured in England and transported the several thousand miles to its new location.

There was a clock in the centre of the building that looked like a miniature Big Ben. It clearly hadn't functioned for some time but, given the somewhat confused nature of arrivals and departures, this seemed appropriate. Behind a small kiosk with a window and a metal grill, a Sudanese official in a black cap sold me a ticket to Wadi Halfa, the last town in the north of the province before Egypt. It was scheduled to depart at ten o'clock the following morning.

'Will it leave on time?' I queried, regretting my question as soon as I had asked it.

He looked at me as if I too had just dropped in from another part of the planet. 'If it does you'll miss it if you're not around to catch it.'

Behind the school was a small hotel. Yes, they had some rooms, the proprietor said. He showed me one that was not much bigger than the small cabin I had just vacated. 'Do you have anything else?' I requested, and was shown to three others that were all the same size, but it was clean, the hotel promised dinner and breakfast and I wasn't in the mood to hunt around.

'So what is there to do in Karima?' I asked, thinking about the twenty four hours ahead of me and the possible few days if the train didn't leave on time.

'You can visit the pyramids in Merowe,' the owner replied, and instructed his nephew to take me where I could find a small boat to ferry me across the river.

Sudan not being Egypt, which had marketed its pyramids so successfully, I expected a small heap of stones vaguely shaped like a triangle and a few pillars to indicate where a temple had once been. But as our small boat rounded a bend in the river there they were: seven perfect pyramids dropped into the middle of the desert as if someone had plucked them from another realm. From that distance they were perfect, spectacular and faintly ridiculous. Why these triangles? What function did they serve, and remembering my history books and the sparse information I had gleaned, were they worth the lives of the thousands of slaves who had built them?

There was an unseemly squabble when a number of 'guides' crowded round to offer their services. They all seemed incredulous when I said I preferred to visit the site on my own.

'It's too far. You'll get lost. There is no water,' they shouted after me, as if I was embarking on some hazardous expedition.

As I began to walk I realized the pyramids were much further away than I had thought. The perspective from the river had concealed their distance and distorted their true scale and size.

I was reluctant to return to the waiting guides, however, wanting neither to look foolish nor to choose between the twenty or thirty unemployed young men eagerly looking for a customer. Fortunately, one of them had detached himself from the group, trailing behind me on his donkey and cart and shouting a range of prices that became progressively lower the more I ignored him.

'Done,' I replied, when he eventually announced something reasonable. I climbed on board, found out that his name was Siddiq and that he came from Karima. I asked him to tell me what he knew about the pyramids of Merowe as we crawled across the desert.

It wasn't much, I discovered, after he had exhausted his description of the place in no more than a few sentences. 'Guide' was something of a misnomer for someone who in effect provided transport, had the foresight to bring water for thirsty travellers and offered, for a few extra Sudanese shillings, some bags of roast peanuts. My book was more informative.

Merowe had once been the centre of a Pharonic kingdom, but the squabbles between two rival dynasties had gradually pushed one of them further and further south beyond what was now the border between Sudan and Egypt. At this place on the river they had established the centre of an empire which had lasted for hundreds of years. As was the way of previous kings these pyramids had been erected to mark their rule and prestige, and to carry them on their journey to the next life when they finished with this one. They were expensive and costly tombs, and not just in terms of the labour required to build them. There was some evidence that several of the kingdoms had bankrupted themselves through the construction of these fabulous monuments, that what posterity had inherited as one of the defining marks of these civilizations had caused their demise.

Up close the pyramids lost much of their symmetry and beauty. Their sides had crumbled and parts of them caved in. Several were full of holes which, Siddiq informed me, marked the place where treasure hunters, archaeologists and casual visitors had entered in search of artefacts. Villagers had also used the stones to construct their houses, he confided, since what was the point in looking elsewhere if they were lying around waiting.

A shabby sign in Arabic warned visitors not to climb up any of them or take away 'the property of the Sudanese Government'. This only added to the air of neglect and indifference, as if the country was uncomfortable with the weight of its history. On some of the pillars that still remained standing, leading up to a temple complex that had disappeared, there was Arabic, English, French, German and even Japanese graffiti. Kilroy had also visited in the late 19th century, according to an inscription etched on one of the columns.

I was surprised, therefore, when we stumbled across a small group of people crawling on their hands and knees over a patch of territory that had been marked out by small flags and bits of string. The leader of this archaeological expedition was a young Frenchman called Thierry. He was there on behalf of some University department in Paris that had been given permission to explore one of the temples. All I could see were small piles of broken pottery scattered over an expanse of sand. If for no other reason than establishing the difference of a few hundred years, however, his expedition had been a success.

He was tolerant of my naive and uninformed questions and seemed happy to show me round the site and explain what they had found. He pointed out the vague outline of buildings and other signs of settlement that were slowly emerging from the desert. The entire area we had traversed by donkey, he said, had a civilization buried beneath it.

I was not surprised to hear that Thierry was 'shocked' by the neglect of this place: the lack of interest by the Government in investing money to protect it and the indifference of the archaeological fraternity to the early civilizations of northern Sudan. The focus of interest was further north in Egypt even though the sites that had been established here were no less important and relevant to their understanding of its history.

'There are two reasons,' he replied, when I asked him why Merowe and other locations in Sudan were of limited interest. The first was to do with marketing. Egypt had managed to develop an entire industry around selling its past. The country's willingness to protect its heritage was closely linked with the revenues this brought in. While archaeological purists complained about the thousands of tourists who scrambled over their sites every year they also realized this industry helped create the infrastructure on which they depended. This included the guards that policed the areas of excavation when they were not around, the museums where the artefacts were displayed and the willingness of the government to give them visas to work in their country.

Sudan was different. Dwarfed by its northern neighbour it had been unable to sell its archaeological heritage to anything like the same extent, and because no revenues were realized it had nothing to invest either in promoting or protecting its past. There was another reason why Sudan was less favoured than Egypt, he continued.

'This place is the entrance to Black Africa. For a long time, many historians and archaeologists believed that nothing of significance came from the rest of the continent. They claimed that northern Sudan was nothing more than a remote outpost of another civilization.'

It had been clear from the hieroglyphs on the Egyptian ruins that considerable commerce had taken place (ostrich feathers, ivory, leopard skins, gold etc), but there was a belief that the cultural traffic was all one way, that civilization moved from north to south and that nothing was reciprocated. 'Why visit Sudan if you believe that the proper, more authentic form of this culture is found in Egypt?'

Thierry went on to tell me about Great Zimbabwe, a civilization 'discovered' in the late 19th century, thousands of miles further south in what would later be called Rhodesia. Early European travellers had located the ruins of a walled city with evidence of iron working, gold production and trade with other continents. Yet such was the persistence of the belief that Africa had no civilization worth speaking of, that the creation of this culture was attributed for many years to early visitors from Egypt. It was only recently that an official acknowledgment was made that Great Zimbabwe was an African achievement.

'We like to believe that we perceive the past through a clear window,' Thierry said, 'but the fact is that prejudice, distortion and cultural biases are there too.'

I left Thierry on his hands and knees, brushing sand away from a corner of a building with a ridiculously small paintbrush. His last words were slightly more optimistic. Several universities in Europe were concerned that the archaeological record of the early civilizations that had emerged in northern Sudan were disappearing. They had 'adopted' various sites in order to conduct excavations such as the one he was on, and to restore some of the ruins so that visitors might come. While the Sudanese Government was far from providing any direct support itself, at least it was not obstructive. The country would never achieve the level of international interest its northern neighbour did, but a considerable amount could still be done to save what was left.

I was not so sure. Back at the river, waiting for the ferry, I was approached by a group of noisy children carrying bags of small, stone carvings, bits of pottery and other artefacts gathered from the nearby pyramids.

They shrugged their shoulders when I asked them if they knew anything about what they were selling, or about the rich history at their doorstep. Quite why people from outside the country would want to buy a small piece of cracked stone or old, broken pottery was beyond them, but it brought them and their families some money. That, in turn, framed the limits of their curiosity and brought to mind Siddiq's almost bland indifference, his few sparse sentences about the place, and his lack of interest in finding out more.

I did not blame any of them for wanting to earn some money. The village the children had emerged from was poor. Their clothes were ragged. The few pennies that the tourists had offered up for these mementos would hardly make them rich. This combination of local poverty, ignorance and the acquisitiveness of outsiders did not offer an encouraging environment for preserving the history of these locations. In the end most of Sudan's rich archaeological heritage, I believed, would probably be exported to museums in London, Paris or New York. Some of it would end up in the drawing rooms of visitors, who had bought a four thousand year old stone relic for a few meagre coins.

'How much of this country will remain behind,' I wondered, as I handed the children a bank note with the President's eyes missing but refused to accept the artefacts offered in return.

The following morning I was wakened by Abdullah tapping at my door. 'I'm not on the ferry any longer,' I remembered, emerging from sleep. 'So why is someone trying to wake me?'

The tapping by that stage had moved to the roof. It got louder and louder as if a group of impatient animals was trotting around upstairs. Then it dawned on me that this was rain such as I had not expected to encounter until I returned home.

What started off as a light irritating shower, however, soon turned into a torrential downpour. The animals upstairs were clearly becoming agitated. We never had rain like this in Scotland. When I looked out of the window I saw that the street outside was submerged. It had been replaced by a river which flowed past the hotel carrying bits of trees along with it.

Above the noise a few minutes later there was a loud, insistent banging at my door and the voice of the proprietor telling me to get out immediately. 'We need to leave now,' he shouted. 'Forget your things.'

As I put on some clothes and grabbed my passport, money and guidebook I had time to think how embarrassing it would be if I drowned in Sudan. Dying of thirst in the desert? Maybe. Perishing at the hands of irate natives or being kicked by a camel would have been more appropriate. Dying in a flash flood in a country which hadn't seen rain for years seemed more ludicrous than unfortunate.

'Come this way,' the proprietor shouted as a group of us scrambled up the hill behind the hotel. A few minutes later we were safe, huddled together with a crowd of people who had fled their homes.

In the early light of morning we could see that the entire neighbourhood was under water. A few dead goats floated past on the river below us. There was a rich smell of mud and wet earth, similar to what I recalled on Muglid's farm. It was as if the Nile had backed up and swallowed everything. With the tops of several houses barely protruding above the water I wondered how many people had lost their lives.

Suddenly it stopped. I had never encountered rain like this nor a downpour turned off so abruptly. One minute it was beating down, threatening an end of the world, and the next second an eerie silence prevailed. As the clouds scurried off into the distance we breathed a sigh of relief, while several people began to pray their thanks for having been spared.

With no rain to sustain it the river began to subside too. 'In ten minutes it will be gone completely,' the proprietor said, 'and then we can go back and see what's happened.'

He told me that rain of this magnitude fell irregularly. 'The last I remember was about ten years ago.' A downpour in the distant hills behind Karima had created a flash flood which swept along the site of an old wadi and into their suburb. It had left several people dead and scores of houses destroyed.

'So why build homes and an hotel in an area of town that is prone to flooding?'

'Every ten years is not too bad,' he replied. 'We take that risk. In any case,' he added, shrugging his shoulders philoso-phically, 'we know now that we are safe for another ten.'

Despite the damage to the houses and the lack of warning, the good news was that no one had been killed. Several goats had been swept away. A lot of property would have to be repaired, but the fact that no one had died seemed to elevate the mood of the people when they contemplated their ruined property.

The hotel was intact, spared the brunt of the flood that had swept past it. There was mud in the front hall, a broken wall on one side, but our rooms were as we had left them, our clothes and belongings not even wet or damp.

'I should have let you sleep,' the proprietor joked when I paid my bill that morning. For the 'inconvenience' of the previous evening, for almost having drowned, he reduced the cost of my stay by a generous twenty five per-cent.

Only two trains a week ran between Karima and Wadi Halfa. My guidebook told me that the first stretch would run beside the river, the railway line weaving in and out of villages and stations, westwards to a place called Abu Hamid. Then there was a long stretch of nothing but desert, a series of hills and a rubbly plain inhabited by a few nomads, their goats and camels. 'Normally it takes one day,' the guidebook said, 'but the train frequently breaks down and so it is best to add a contingency to the length of your journey.'

Despite my doubts that any transport in Sudan would ever arrive at its appointed place at the right time, the train was there, the large engine spewing out a cloud of black smoke while a long snake of dilapidated carriages trailed behind it. The entire town seemed to have turned out either to travel or to say goodbye. Not completely comfortable with having to push and shove against the crowd I made slow progress towards my carriage. 'Don't bother,' someone advised. No one respected the numbers they had been given and the best thing to do was to spot an empty seat and grab it.

'Why don't you join us,' Mahmud said, as he motioned his wife and four daughters to make room for me on their bench. Squeezed together like friendly sardines they were on their way to Egypt where he had found work. I was slotted between Mahmud and his oldest daughter, Fawzia, who led the rest of her sisters in a chorus of giggles whenever they contemplated the foreigner they had adopted. Truth to tell I came to appreciate Fawzia's considerable size, since she provided a comfortable cushion to soften the bumping and jolting once we left the station.

The Sudanese, as I had discovered, love to travel. Despite the discomfort of being packed together, despite the sand and dust that blew in through the open windows, despite the frequent halts and delays, there was an air of festivity in the carriage, as if everyone was determined to have a good time. People chatted to each other like long lost friends. Food and water and babies were shared and passed around to strangers. No one complained. When the train ground to a halt for an hour to make some repairs, people shrugged their shoulders and muttered 'Inshallah'.

Watching the people around me, their easy manner and

familiarity with each other, I remembered the journeys I had made as a child. Every year during our summer holidays we would embark on a long journey by rail and sea from our home in Scotland to our relatives in Germany. The moment we entered our carriage, our parents and the people around us were transformed, as if the journey ahead relaxed their inhibitions.

Usually reserved, aloof and distant, my father would strike up conversations with strangers and relate stories about his exploits at sea. My mother would relate our family history and swap addresses that we knew would later be discarded. It was the journey itself we looked forward to, as much as our arrival in another country. The shifting scenery outside the window, the lights of the different cities and their exotic names intrigued us as we flashed past them enclosed in our moving bubble. Maybe we are all nomads at heart, I reflected, and our natural inclination is not to sit still or stay in one place but to swap locations and move on. Maybe that is why travel liberates us and makes us more sociable.

'What do you think of my daughters?' Mahmud interrupted my thoughts a short while later. The girls had been laughing continuously ever since we left Karima and regularly shifted around to take their turn beside me. Under the watchful eye of their mother they clearly enjoyed my embarrassment every time the train gave a sudden lurch that threw us together.

'They're very nice,' I replied, confused by the question and wondering what else I could possibly have said.

'Fawzia should be married soon,' he continued, and asked her to remove her shawl so I could see her properly. I found it difficult to believe that the woman in front of me was only sixteen years old.

'Isn't it best that she wait a few years before she gets married?' I replied. There was another burst of laughter from the girls, the mother, Mahmud and a small group of people who had tuned into our conversation.

'What about you, Mr. Chris? Aren't you married yet?' Mahmud asked.

I shook my head and said I was too young, that I didn't

want to get married until my thirties when I would be more responsible and able to support a family. This occasioned a gasp of surprise from the crowd that had gathered. I had had these conversations before with the teachers at school. People in Sudan got married when they could and 'when they could' meant having the money to pay the bride price and the costs of the wedding. As a teacher and a foreigner I must have plenty of money. So what could possibly be holding me back?

'What about Fawzia?' Mahmud continued with a straight face, so I could not be sure if he was joking or not. 'You are a good man. You have a good job. My daughter needs to get married. She is strong. She will have many children. The only problem is that you're not a Muslim.'

Not being a Muslim was always my means of escape, the obstacle that always came up whenever this subject was discussed. 'Oh, what a pity,' I responded. 'I'd love to marry your daughter, but unfortunately I'm a Christian, and Muslims and Christians can't get married, can they?'

'You can always convert!' Mahmud persisted, encouraged now by a large crowd of onlookers.

Fawzia seemed indifferent to this speculation about her future. She was cracking sunflower seeds between her teeth in company with her sisters, as if this discussion about a potential husband was no more important a topic than what they might have for breakfast.

Pretending a religious conviction I did not posses I said that conversion was not so easy, that for someone to abandon their own religion and embrace another required a lot of consideration, more reflection than was possible during a bumpy train ride in the north of Sudan.

'La Illaha Ill 'Allah, Mohammed ar Rasul Allah' someone in the carriage shouted. 'Get him to say these words.' This was the Muslim creed. 'There is no God but God and Mohammed is his prophet.' My colleagues at school had spent endless hours trying to get me to say it, as if the simple pronouncement of this sentence would be sufficient to save my soul.

'I'll have to think about it,' I replied, as graciously as I could, trying to find a way of not offending anyone. I had never been entirely comfortable with this kind of banter, wondering how serious everyone was about this subject and aware of the fraught history and misconceptions that characterized the relationship between our respective religions.

Despite the joking that took place on the subject of my conversion I could detect at times an edge to the discussions that made me wary. An inappropriate remark, an ill thought response might easily cause an offence that would turn into an argument. 'What's the big deal?' someone had once said to me. 'We never see you pray. You never read the Bible. You never go to church. You say you're a Christian but where's the proof? If your own religion is not that important to you why not convert to ours?'

I could always have said I was an atheist, of course, but I had seen the reaction to Arthur's statement one day when he had confessed that he didn't believe in God to a group of colleagues. Being a bad Christian was infinitely preferable to being a committed non-believer. That much was clear. Arthur had subsequently said that attitudes changed towards him after he made this confession.

Thankfully, the topic was brought to a close by the announcement of our imminent arrival in Abu Hamid. This was the station where the train would split. Half the people would head south towards Khartoum while the rest of us would head north towards Wadi Halfa. Mahmud cautioned me to stay alert and follow his lead. We would have to change carriages. There would be another scramble for seats, he warned, and the journey north across the desert was even more uncomfortable than the one we had just completed.

We had stopped at several settlements on the first part of our journey from Karima. Never very far from the river, the railway line had tracked a line of trees and vegetation that pushed the desert to a discreet distance. But once past Abu Hamid, we struck northwards away from these settlements and soon entered a bleak and barren plain that was as intimidating as anything I had seen. The mood in the carriage seemed to shift. The landscape we passed through provoked a quieter, more reflective mood than the boisterous first part of our journey.

My guidebook enthused about the track we were traversing, not because of the comfort of our ride but because of the feat of engineering that had made it possible. It was built to accommodate Kitchener's army, the one that avenged the death of General Gordon and brought to an end Sudan's brief flirtation with independence in the 19th century.

According to my book, because of the poor navigability of large sections of the Nile, Kitchener had been faced with a dilemma in transporting his troops southwards from Egypt. Ignoring the advice of engineers, politicians and other advisors he went ahead and built 360 kilometres of railway line over an unexplored and waterless desert in a period of only 5 months and at the hottest time of the year. Able to transport troops, munitions, heavy guns and 'an endless supply of whisky, soda water, cigarettes and sausages', to keep up the morale of his soldiers, the Sudanese army was roundly defeated south of Abu Hamid.

Did Mahmud appreciate the irony of utilizing a means of transport that had brought to an end his country's first attempt at liberation? No, he had never heard that story before and spat out of the window to show his solidarity with the defeated Mahdist forces. Pointing out that the alternative journey would take over a week, by boat to Dongola and then north across the stony terrain of northern Nubia, he confided, 'I'll still come this way in future even though you've illuminated our past.'

Sandwiched between his friendly daughters, my face wrapped in a scarf to protect me from the dust that swirled through the carriage, I soon fell asleep. It was Mahmud who woke me some time later, nudging me in the ribs and pointing to a figure that had appeared at the end of our carriage. He was dressed in rags and as he shuffled down the aisle towards us people parted to let him pass, digging into their bags at the same time to offer him some money.

I had seen beggars before. In general, people treated them with a kind of tolerant irritation. 'It's a religious duty to help them,' Abdel Majid had told me, 'but in a country where most people are poor it isn't done with any great enthusiasm.'

This one seemed to command considerably more respect, judging by the way people made room for him and thrust money into his hands even though he never wheedled or cajoled like the others. 'That's because he's special,' Mahmud whispered, as he dug into his pockets to hand me a coin. 'It's bad luck if you don't give him something.'

There were lots of stories that circulated about 'the mad man of Karima.' The one that Mahmud thought was the most likely was that he came from a relatively poor family in that town and had fallen in love with a rich neighbour's daughter. They had been caught 'together' one evening and the woman had been sent away to live with another part of her family. 'Generally if these things happen in our society, the parents find a compromise and the couple get married,' Mahmud said. 'But it seems the rich neighbour wasn't interested in giving his permission.'

The rumoured sequel to this drama was that the woman had killed herself and her lover had gone mad with grief. Now dressed in rags, he had spent the last few years travelling on trains, seemingly oblivious of their direction and destination. People fed him. They gave him money. I remarked that given the circumstances of his history, an affair outside marriage, I would have thought people would have been more censorious.

'We all make mistakes,' Mahmud replied. 'In any case, God will make whatever judgment is necessary, not us.'

There was something scary in the fixed expression of the person who worked his way down the carriage towards us. His clothes were torn. His hair was dishevelled. He smelt terribly too, as if he had never had a bath or shower since he first embarked on his endless travels. 'Barak Allah Fiq,' he muttered, when I dropped my coins into his hand. 'God bless you.' These words were uttered automatically, as if there was no one behind them, as if the person who occupied the physical space in front of us had long since departed.

'At least we haven't offended him,' Mahmud whispered

after he had passed. 'You never know. Maybe the things they say about him are true.'

By the middle of the afternoon the heat was at its most intense. The open windows offered no relief but invited instead a cloud of sand and hot air to blow through the carriage, forcing us all to wrap our shawls more tightly around our heads. Memories of my bus journey some months earlier came flooding back, although this time I was better prepared. 'Do you want to go outside?' Mahmud asked me.

'To run after the train?'

'Not quite,' he laughed. 'Follow me.'

On the side of our carriage was a series of metal steps that led up to the roof. According to Mahmud it was much cooler 'on top' and we would have a better view.

'Isn't it dangerous?' I asked as he pulled himself through the open window.

'Not at all. I do this all the time.'

So did several others. On the top of our carriage a small group of people were gathered together, holding on to whatever footholds and protrusions they could find. A space was made for us beside a group of young men. They seemed amused that a 'Khawadja' had decided to join them, but solicitous too as they pointed out where I had to hold on and how to balance myself when we came to a bend and the train lurched to one side.

'Has anyone ever fallen off?' I asked Mahmud, once I had a firm hold.

'Someone I was once travelling with fell asleep but I grabbed him before he fell. Stay awake and you'll be fine.'

From our elevation we had a better view of the landscape. The guidebook had done it complete justice, stating it was probably the bleakest railway line in the world. Once or twice we spotted a well in the distance, a small herd of goats and an occasional camel, but people were nowhere to be seen.

Alongside the track there was a string of old telephone poles. The bits of wire between them had long since disappeared. They had been blunted and carved by the wind into strange shapes and the wood bleached the colour of sand. Stretching for miles ahead and behind us they only heightened the feeling of desolation. They were probably as old as Kitchener's army, I speculated, imagining at the same time the message of triumph they had once communicated to a waiting empire anxious for revenge.

When the light softened as we moved into late afternoon the landscape around us became transformed. The sand glowed a range of different colours. Shadows softened the contours of hills so that for a while it was easy to imagine the place was friendlier than I knew it really was. Some of the writers whose journeys through the desert I had read had remarked on its hostility, its indifference, the hardships and suffering that accompanied their journeys to wild places. But they had also spoken of its attraction, how at the end of a long day's march and with the light falling in a particular way it became a place of incredible beauty. For a while I could see what they meant and understand their fascination with a landscape that frightened and intrigued them at the same time.

It was Mahmud who stirred me from my reverie some time later. 'We'd best go down now,' he said. It was getting dark and the lights that flickered in the distance were those of Wadi Halfa. This was the end of the railway line and the place from which most of the passengers would embark by ferry across Lake Aswan to Egypt.

I refused Mahmud's invitation to join him and his family on their journey to Cairo, where he assured me I would get a job every bit as prestigious as the one I had in Sudan. There was my school to return to. I had not yet 'finished' with Dongola, and despite the pleasurable disposition of his daughters I was not quite ready to settle down and get married.

7

Into the Belly of Stones

Like everyone else on the train Mahmud, his wife and daughters made their way towards the ferry at the edge of the lake that would take them to Egypt. The people had been at the station when we arrived, workers returning home to Sudan, were going south. The crowd I had been travelling with was heading north. No one it seemed was destined for Wadi Halfa itself and after a walk around town I understood why.

Wadi Halfa had once been a prosperous settlement on the Nile, originally a staging post for the Ottoman and the later British invasions of the country. But when Aswan Dam was constructed several hundred kilometres downstream in the 1950's, to provide Egypt with electricity, the water backed up all the way to Wadi Halfa and beyond.

Much of the original town; the houses, the farms, the date plantations, the mosques and churches, the historical ruins of ancient Nubia, had been flooded. What was left was the shell of a community and a lake with scores of villages and a good deal of history beneath it. The benefits of cheap electricity, better irrigation, flood mitigation and tourism had been captured by the Egyptians further south. Wadi Halfa was a casualty.

Omar had previously been a teacher in the town at one of its principal secondary schools. Now he was the proprietor of a small store that overlooked a market which had clearly seen better days. There was none of the usual buzz, chatter and excitement I had witnessed so many times before. A few stalls displayed dates, lemons and some tired looking fish taken from the lake.

'We were moved to another part of Sudan when the water reached the town,' he said, eager to answer my questions and share the experience.

Had anyone asked them what they wanted?

'No one. We were told that this was how it would be, that we would have no say in what would happen to us.'

His family was moved and settled in Gezira province, in the cotton triangle of central Sudan. They received a small house, a plot of land, some start-up capital for cotton production and a mosquito net. Other families were settled further east near the border with Ethiopia and what had once been a community became fragmented and scattered through different parts of the country.

'The mosquitoes were terrible. Malaria was common. None of us were used to growing cotton. The people in the villages nearby didn't like us either. They said we were outsiders and that we had stolen their land.'

With a few other families, Omar returned a few years later to see if they could resurrect something of their old community.

He acknowledged that it was not easy, that the heart of the town had been ripped out and its economy ruined. 'There is nothing much for us to do here now,' he confessed, as we watched a group of boys at the edge of the market tormenting a donkey with a wooden stick. 'But hard though it is, it is better than where we were.'

He was resentful of how the governments of Sudan and Egypt had ignored the strong allegiance of the people to their homeland. They had assumed that financial compensation and offering them a new place to live would somehow make up for their lost history and culture.

'Many of us got sick down there and it wasn't just malaria. Some said that our ancestors were angry, that they were calling us to return.'

I admired Omar's resolve and the determination of those who had come back to restore something of what they had lost. It also brought home to me for the first time, even though I had read about this before, the sometimes cavalier attitude of development planners to the welfare of people affected by their grand schemes and projects. Was Aswan Dam worth the ruined livelihoods of thousands of people, the destruction of their communities, the flooding of ancient civilizations that were among the first in recorded history?

Omar told me there was increasing evidence that the lake was silting up. The farmers in Egypt had become dependent on chemical fertilizers once they no longer had the annual floods from the Nile to replenish their soil. The sardine industry had also been affected, ruining the livelihoods of thousands of fishermen in the northern part of that country. The children who swam in the lake now had bilharzia because the water was stagnant. Malaria was more common. There had clearly been a cost to the construction of one of Africa's technological wonders and, as usual, it was the poor who had suffered the most.

Wadi Halfa was hot and dusty. There were few trees to provide shade or anchor the soil that blew around. There were clouds of flies in the market, settling over everyone and everything. The station in the centre of town seemed to invite departure rather than arrival. It was by far the most depressing location I had seen in the time I had been in Sudan, even more depressing than the shanty town on the edge of Khartoum that John had shown me.

Unfortunately, there was little traffic in the direction I was going and Omar warned me that I might have to wait several days before I could leave.

'Don't be so eager to take off,' he remarked, noticing my look of dismay. The track south of Wadi Halfa passed through a stony desert called 'The Belly of Stones' and if I thought the journey had been arduous so far then I was about to experience something even more difficult.

'It's as rough as hell,' the guidebook confirmed, and given its normally bland observations this description did nothing to allay my concerns as to what lay ahead.

Sipping tea at his shop two mornings later, Omar announced that he had found me a ride on the back of a lorry heading south. 'It will go all the way to Dongola,' he said as I thanked him, 'but will probably stop at all the villages in between.'

It was transporting dates, which are not very comfortable to sit or lie on, especially if they are dry and hard. After a time they feel likes stones, forcing you to move around every few minutes to find a more comfortable position.

'But they are better than metal pipes,' one of my fellow travellers offered in consolation, as we bumped and jolted along a track that followed the river into northern Nubia.

This remark prompted a discussion about the best load to travel on, since in many parts of the country where buses, taxis, ferries and planes didn't operate, hitching a lift on the back of a lorry was the only form of transport. Someone had once caught a lift on a truck transporting mattresses across the desert. 'I slept most of the way,' he said, which didn't improve the mood among the rest of us as we continued our journey.

The driver of the truck had been apologetic, since he had no space in the front cabin to accommodate me. It turned out that the passenger who had deprived me of a more comfortable place was another expatriate teacher. Ron was in his mid thirties, covered his face with a thick beard and had a strong South African accent, which turned out to be Rhodesian. He had taught for over a year in the town of Atbara further south and, like me, was exploring the country while the Ministry of Education worked out a compromise with its employees.

He seemed reserved in front of our effusive Sudanese colleagues and refused the tea that was always offered during the frequent breaks in our journey. As I had discovered, shared hardships are always a good way of breaking down social barriers and I wondered what kept him so distant and un-willing to engage in the banter and conversation of his fellow travellers.

Bit by bit, however, he began to disclose more about himself, sometimes seeking out my company on the edge of our group. I knew that his country was at war, its small group of privileged whites trying to maintain their status at the expense of the African population. Ron had been in the armed forces, in a special unit called the Selous Scouts that was involved in counter insurgency.

'Don't ask,' he replied, when I asked him what this involved.

He went on to tell me that he became fed up with the killings, the atrocities and the pointlessness of a war that was always going to be lost. 'It's their land after all. It belongs to them,' although the way he said 'their land' and 'them' indicated an attitude of resentment that had still not left him, that had not been completely abandoned when he had fled his country to come here.

So what was he doing in Sudan, in the middle of a continent he seemed to disparage, doing good works and living in conditions that must have been even more basic than the ones he left behind?

'Making reparations,' he replied, and though I thought he was joking at first, I could see from his straight face and demeanour that he was serious, that he was here on a personal mission to somehow make up for the behaviour of his people in Africa.

Coming to Sudan had been a revelation, he continued. It had opened his eyes to a lot of things he had never expected. The friendship and warmth of the community he had found himself in contradicted what his upbringing had told him, that Africans were insular, unfriendly and suspicious. There was the rich history of the Nile he had discovered and the indigenous Sudanese cultures that had surprised him. While Africans might be loyal, obedient and occasionally hard working, the stereotype he carried around with him excluded any appreciation of their own history. Like Thierry he mentioned Great Zimbabwe and the unwillingness of his countrymen to believe that it was a civilization built by local people.

'So why this distance and awkwardness?' I asked him, 'this attitude you show to the Sudanese we are travelling with? Do you find it difficult to relate to them?'

'Yes, I do,' he replied, looking regretful and disappointed with himself. 'No matter what you do to escape, your past never quite leaves you.'

At the start of the strike he had been invited to spend some time with the family of a fellow teacher in one of the rural villages near Atbara. They were generous to a fault, he confessed, but part of him still felt uncomfortable, 'almost as if I had a revulsion to being so close, to sharing their company.' He made his excuses and left, worried that he might say something that would offend them, of doing something that might betray his feelings.

'I suppose I'm not ready for this experience,' he said, 'and perhaps I never will be.'

Part of me was shocked by Ron's frank disclosure of the prejudice he carried around with him. At the start of our journey he had made a disparaging remark about my local attire, the fact that it was inappropriate for a European to be wearing such clothes. I had heard too in the short, curt answers he offered our Sudanese companions whenever they spoke to him, something of the attitudes he had hoped to leave behind, but I felt too that Ron was genuinely conflicted, uneasy with himself and resentful towards the society that had formed his values. In his own way he was trying to move on, to embrace an experience that would change him for the better.

Though never as much a victim as the people he had been taught to look down on, something harmful had been done to him too. 'Be patient,' I counselled. 'These things take time.'

Khalid, our driver, preferred to travel at night when it was cooler and the lights of the vehicle could better pick out obstacles and potholes on the track ahead of us. But cool in the cabin meant something different on the back of a lorry. Over and above the hard dates we bumped around on, we had the discomfort of being bitterly cold.

Sometime in the late evening we were flagged down by some travellers at the side of the road, waving a lamp to attract our attention. They were going to the next village and after some haggling with the driver, four men got on board carrying a long, heavy carpet which they hoisted up on to the lorry and stowed at the back. They joined our group, huddling under the tent of blankets, clothes and baggage we had erected around ourselves and there was the usual exchange of greetings, most of it in a language I did not understand.

They were Nubians, one of them replied when I asked what they were speaking. Their dialect seemed different from the Dongolawi I had become familiar with. There were several dialects, he explained, and although they were related there were differences as well. The one they spoke was called Mahas, common in the area south of Wadi Halfa. I pointed to the three wide scars he had on the side of his face, and asked him if this was also a defining feature of his people.

'Yes,' he said, 'In Dongola the same scars are found in a different position. Near Kerma, where there is another group of Nubians, the scarring is different again.'

A few hours and a lot of bumping around later we pulled into their village. 'I hope you will spend the rest of the night as our guests,' one of them announced. 'It is surely too cold for you to continue.'

I was tired, bruised, hungry and desperate for sleep. Would the driver, who had only been kept awake with numerous cups of strong tea, agree to rest for a while? Thankfully he was tired and hungry too and switched off the engine to accept their offer.

We were not the only ones invited, it seemed. Near the place where we had stopped the lights of several fires illuminated a large number of people. The noise of our arrival had obviously stirred them. Within a few minutes we were surrounded, although the welcome was not the one I would have expected. Many of the women were sobbing, their cries and ululations piercing the night air.

'Have you just returned from a long journey?' I asked one of the new passengers. 'Is this a reception committee to welcome you home?'

'No,' he replied,' we are here to bury my brother.'

As they lifted the carpet from the back of the truck to hand it down to the people who waited below a foot emerged from one end and a hand from another and I realized that one of our travelling companions had been a dead body.

'How else were they supposed to transport him?' Khalid

replied when I asked if he had known we had been travelling with a corpse. 'I could hardly refuse to take him.'

The villagers were friendly, solicitous and constantly concerned about our welfare. From somewhere a rug was produced for Ron and me to lie on. Despite the late hour food was prepared and lots of sweet tea. A bottle of arak, date wine, was also passed around. It was every bit as rough as I had been told to expect, although for a while it kept out the cold and deadened the pain of our bruises.

We were a source of curiosity to the children who edged up to the light of the fire. The arrival of the dead man was clearly a village event, providing an excuse for them to escape the attention of their parents. Cautious at first we could hear their laughter and whispers whenever we spoke or made a movement. Our popularity rocketed when Ron produced some chocolate, divided it into small pieces and handed it round.

'Let them get some sleep,' one of the brothers we had travelled with earlier said as he chased the children away. Again he apologized for not offering us the guest room in their house. That was where the dead man was lying and where his body was being prepared for the funeral the next day.

'What we have is good enough,' I thanked him, expressing our appreciation of the way in which we had been made so welcome and how the villagers had shared with us the little they had. Ron nodded his head too and in tolerable Arabic, that he had never let on he knew, asked him to communicate our thanks for the hospitality we had received. I was glad to see him so relaxed and appreciative of what had been done for us. Perhaps he was more ready to interact with this country and its people than I had earlier thought.

Khalid, who had slept in the back of his truck all night, joined us for breakfast the following morning. Having accepted the hospitality of the village, he said, it was only right that we attend the funeral of the dead man. The ceremony would probably begin soon, he added. The custom was always to have a quick burial.

Since the temperature during the middle of the day could

reach as high as forty five degrees in this part of the country, it was clear that this tradition made sense.

When the body was finally brought out, wrapped in a simple white shroud, the women in the crowd began the long, piercing wail, the keening, that had greeted us the previous evening. The men were more sedate, walking behind the body with their hands outstretched and reciting prayers from the Koran. I was unsure of what we should do. Should we walk behind? Would our presence as Christians in a Muslim funeral be resented? 'Not at all,' one of the brothers said. 'You are both welcome.'

The grave-yard was some distance away, on a small hill overlooking the river and the village. I wondered if it reflected the straitened circumstances of the community since it was modest and almost indistinguishable from the ground on which it was set. Small, upright stones marked previous burials. The only exception was a cone-shaped hut made out of bricks and plaster. I knew without asking that this must be the tomb of a local saint, since it looked exactly like the one Muglid had shown me a few months previously.

The grave of the man we were burying was dug into the ground to a shallow depth. The hard, gravelly terrain at the edge of the village did not permit anything deeper. Flat stones were put on top of the body when it was lowered into place to prevent the wild dogs and jackals from digging the body up and devouring it later.

The ceremony itself was a quick and simple affair. There were a few words said by some of the villagers about the merits of the dead man and some final prayers led by the Imam who presided over the occasion. It was the women in the background who continued to provide the emotional content and atmosphere. They had kept up their wailing ever since we had left the house, some of them beating their breasts and tearing at their clothes in a public display of grief.

As we walked back towards the village, the wife and children of the dead man came over to thank us for our presence at the funeral. They were touched that strangers from another country had come to pay their respects. 'Stay as long as you wish,' they said, indicating that the ceremonies would continue for almost a week, since people from the neighbouring villages who had not yet arrived would also have to be hosted.

By the time Khalid said that it was time for us to leave it was already late afternoon. After a delay of over a day I wondered what the rest of our fellow travellers thought about the interruption of their journey. Ron and I were happy to have stayed. We had time on our hands and were curious too, but what about the businessmen who wanted to sell their dates at the market in Dongola? That was an event they would now miss. There was the soldier returning to his regiment. Would he be reprimanded for being late? Everyone apart from us had schedules to keep and a timetable to follow. But when I asked them the reply was the same.

'No one gets impatient when someone dies. It could be any of us being buried back there.'

Among the instructions we had received in Khartoum was a set of precautions that we should observe in order to maintain our health. 'Don't drink unsafe water! If you are unsure where it has come from, boil it! Don't eat uncooked vegetables! Beware of fresh tomatoes and cucumbers!' Whoever had written these warnings could not have travelled in the country or lived outside the city where these precautions were sensible.

Water was in short supply on the dry, dusty roads of northern Sudan. The few bottles you might carry were soon empty. The only alternative on offer was water carried in old goat skins on the side of the lorry or raised from a village well whenever you happened to stumble across one. At the same time, there was precious little wood in the desert to light a fire and boil anything. So, in general, you did what the Sudanese did whenever they were thirsty. You said a prayer before you took a swig and hoped that what you found had no bugs in it. 'Thirst can kill you too,' I reckoned.

Contaminated water contained amoebas. Invisible to the naked eye, they were quite at home in your stomach where they secreted nasty toxins that made you ill. Dysentery was a common topic of discussion among expatriate teachers. 'Don't worry,' George had said in London. 'You will learn what dysentery is soon enough.'

Whether it was the brackish water I had drunk in Wadi Halfa or the vegetables I had eaten at the funeral I found myself on the back of the lorry that evening with terrible stomach cramps. This rapidly progressed into an immediate and urgent need to go to the toilet. Ron was solicitous, offering up his seat in the front of the lorry so I could be more comfortable. He knew what was in store. 'The first time is the worst', he said. 'You just want to roll over and die, but don't worry, antibiotics will cure it within a few days.'

The rest of the group was patient with me too. Added to our regular stops for tea were my own frantic requests to halt our journey so I could relieve myself. Not a word of disapproval or criticism was uttered as I stumbled off into the desert for some privacy, sometimes returning more than half an hour later.

Clearly I could not continue. One of the merchants travelling to Dongola had an uncle in the next town, with whom I could stay. There was a clinic there too. I nodded my head when this option was proposed, happy to hand over such decisions. My only preoccupation was how I would get through the next few hours.

We pulled up outside a house in Kerma just as the first light of morning broke over the town. With a minimum of fuss or any need for prolonged explanations, I was taken to a room and shown a direct line to the toilet. The rest of the group was provided with tea and breakfast, but as soon as they had finished they decided to continue. The merchants were getting nervous about missing another market and the soldier was keen to return too.

In my haggard state I was unable to offer much more than a few cursory farewells to the people who had looked after me so well. When I thanked Ron for his support and the company I had come to enjoy, he seemed touched by these words and promised to keep in contact. He also apologized for the remarks he had made about the clothes I was wearing when we had first met.

'Maybe the next time I see you I'll be dressed in native gear as well,' he said, before waving goodbye.

Othman was the head of the household I found myself in and once again I was struck by the Sudanese capacity for genuine hospitality and friendliness. A few words from his nephew were enough of an introduction. I was welcomed into his family, given the best room in the house and extended all the courtesy and attention I could have wished for.

In the middle of the morning he woke me up from a fitful sleep and drove me to the clinic. Obviously a person of some influence, he negotiated a path through the other patients who had probably been waiting for several hours. I was ushered into the presence of the district doctor, who took one look at me and pronounced that I had amoebic dysentery.

Confirmed by a stool test a short while later, he told me it was simple enough to cure. The tablets I would need to take were unpleasant and would make me nauseous. I had heard of Flagyll. Some teachers carried bottles of it in their bags when they travelled. Said to be as bad as the illness it cured, I would have to take them three times a day for the next week. Although I might notice a substantial improvement in the next few days, I would still have to complete the course. 'If you don't eliminate it completely, dysentery will come back even worse than before.'

Othman brushed aside my apologies for the inconvenience I had caused and the disruption of my sudden, unannounced arrival. 'Don't worry,' he said, as we drove back to his home. 'You can stay as long as you need.'

Both he and his family were considerate hosts. They prepared food when I was hungry, supplied me with regular cups of tea and soup, and left me alone when I needed to rest. His sons were students attending the boy's secondary school in Dongola. Like the rest of us they had no idea when their education might resume. As part payment for the hospitality I received I offered them some English lessons when I had the energy to do so.

Othman traded dates and other produce in the district, an

occupation that brought him a comfortable living and left him with considerable time on his hands. He was a devout Muslim, attended prayers in the mosque every day and was a member of one of the local Tariqas, the Sufi orders that Muglid had once talked about.

His other passion was local history and he had accumulated a considerable library of academic papers and books on the subject of Nubia and the early civilizations along this part of the Nile. Like Thierry he resented the fact that much of this history had been ignored, that civilizations this far up the river were perceived as nothing more than an appendage of Egypt. As soon as I was able to walk around without having to be in close proximity to the nearest toilet, he invited me to see some of the historical sites around town.

According to Othman Kerma had one of the most illustrious pasts of all the settlements in northern Sudan. I found it difficult to believe that this sleepy town of a few thousand people had had such a prestigious history. An early settlement had sprung up along this part of the Nile as far back as 3,000 BC. The kingdom of Kush had its heyday about a thousand years later, when Egypt was in turmoil. Kerma's rulers had pushed north and south to create a Nubian kingdom that rivalled anything in the region. This civilization had lasted for almost five hundred years, until an Egyptian army had finally marched into the territory, killed the king and his family and ended its period of glory.

As we drove out of town Othman pointed to a hill in the distance that rose abruptly from the surrounding plain. I had thought this was a natural feature of the landscape until he told me that it was a temple complex established by the early rulers of Kerma. Called a Defuffa, of which there were several in the area, it was made of mud brick and covered a huge expanse of ground. With its eroded walls and red, sandy colour it seemed more organic than manmade.

Although its purpose was still being debated, evidence pointed to a more sinister function. Inside the Defuffa, the tombs of several kings had been excavated and it was clear from these that Kerma had developed a strong tradition of

funerary sacrifice. In one of the digs that Othman had participated in, the remains of several hundred people had been
found, with evidence to show they had all been killed. The
remains of horses, cattle and dogs had also been found and it
was widely believed they had been sacrificed to ensure that the
king, or head of some prestigious family, had company on his
passage to the next life.

'It's an impressive but extremely brutal way to pay your last
respects,' Othman observed.

My tour for the day was not quite over. As we proceeded
further out of town Othman said that he wanted to show me
some more contemporary ruins. I had supposed we were going
to visit some of the Egyptian temples that my guidebook had
talked about. There were lots of them around Kerma too.

An hour later on the edge of where the belt of vegetation
along the river met the desert proper, I was presented instead
with a large area of empty sand. I could see nothing at first
until Othman pointed out where some bits of rusty metal
protruded above the ground. This was what was left of an
agricultural project that had been established only a few years
previously. It had been designed to convert an area south of
Kerma into a huge garden, which would not only supply the
province with the vegetables it needed, but other parts of
the country as well. Funded by a consortium of banks, the
Sudanese Government and some international donors, it had
turned into a white elephant only a short while after it had
been constructed. All that remained was the twisted metal of
abandoned machinery.

'We told the engineers when they came here that it wouldn't
work,' Othman explained. 'The farmers who knew the area
said that the soil, the climate, the location just wasn't right. But
by that stage nothing was going to stop them. We sat back and
watched them make fools of themselves.'

I asked Othman the same question I had asked Omar in
Wadi Halfa, whether anyone had bothered to consult them, or
listen to their opinions. He shook his head in the same way and
I was reminded too of Muglid's description of the attitude of
the experts sent to help them. Dismissive, unresponsive and at

times contemptuous their assumption seemed to be that the farmers who had lived along the river for centuries had nothing worthwhile to offer in terms of information and experience. Indigenous people were there to listen, to learn and to accept everything that was thrown at them. That was all.

Like most people in the society I came from I was happy to contribute my occasional few shillings to collection boxes for third world development whenever they were put in front of me. I had read too about the millions of pounds provided in overseas aid. I had assumed that the projects this generosity supported must all be success stories, but over the course of the past few days I had witnessed two schemes which had failed utterly. They shocked me and made me realize for the first time that development was something much more complex than a simple transfer of money, skills and machinery to poor people in poor countries.

Othman nodded his head when I asked him whether he and his people were angry about the kinds of programme that did not take their views, opinions and experience into account.

'The worst thing is that although our families have been living here for thousands of years our opinions don't seem to matter. Development is perceived as something done to us rather than a process we should participate in.'

A few days later I waved goodbye to Othman and his family. His boys were travelling with me since we had heard on the radio that schools would resume in a few days time. A deal had been struck that the teachers and the Ministry of Education could both live with, until the following year at least.

On the hard, bumpy track south I had time to reflect on the places I had visited over the past few weeks and the people I had met. Although I felt guilty about being away from work for so long, I realized that my own education had benefitted immensely, that my own schooling had taken place during the period I was away. I had tried as much as possible to leave my preconceptions behind and embrace what the country had to offer. In return, I had encountered hospitality, friendship, a sense of community, a vibrant and intriguing culture, an immensely rich history and most importantly perhaps, a jolt to the superficiality that characterized many of the views on Africa I carried around with me.

Dongola was the same as I remembered when we caught sight of it in the distance. As we approached, I saw the belt of palm trees that surrounded it and the tops of the minarets protruding above them. Closer in, I could see the bend on the river it overlooked and the fluttering sails of the feluccas on the Nile that I loved to watch from Hassan's coffee house. While the town was familiar, I felt that I had traded my naïvety for something more insightful about the country I was living in. It had only been two weeks since I had left but I felt it wasn't the same teacher who was now returning.

8

Return to Khartoum

I had been in Dongola for six months and had yet to be paid. Apparently there had been a mix up with my papers in Khartoum which meant that as far as the Ministry was concerned I didn't officially exist.

'Don't worry,' everyone said. 'It will soon be sorted out,' a reassurance I treated with suspicion whenever the word 'soon' was used. I survived on the charity of my fellow teachers and lines of credit opened up for me in town, but as the weeks and months dragged on, I grew worried I would acquire a reputation.

'I will repay you tomorrow,' began to sound like 'I will repay you never.' I was working. I deserved to be paid. Would I complete my contract without receiving a penny?

'There is a way you can sort this whole thing out,' an official at the provincial office told me. 'Go back to Khartoum. Register again and you'll get your money,' which made me wonder why this advice hadn't been offered in the first place.

John lent me the cost of the bus fare to Khartoum and Arthur gave me some funds to tide me over while I sorted out my business.

'If you don't get paid, don't come back', they said. 'Half the town won't speak to you.'

I was better prepared for my journey south than when I had first come to Dongola. I had a scarf to cover my head, bottles of water, dried dates, a blanket and a bottle of Flagyll in case I contracted dysentery. What I wasn't prepared for was our arrival in Khartoum. After six months in remote and placid northern Sudan it was a large, confusing and intimidating metropolis. There was traffic everywhere, crowds of people scurrying around, shops selling everything, beggars at street corners pushing and shoving, and women conversing with men in public and showing more than a discreet ankle.

I felt like a country bumpkin arriving in the city for the first time. On this occasion, however, no one offered to adopt me. Perhaps with my dirty clothes, my shawl and headscarf I gave the impression of a person familiar with the country, of someone who didn't need looking after.

'Your document has been ready for some time,' an official in the Ministry of Education told me when I enquired about my salary the next day.

He was partly hidden behind a stack of folders on his desk. There were piles more in the corners and on the floor, anywhere there was space to dump them, and I noticed, with alarm, that some of the folders were even propping up a leg of the desk.

'Don't worry. I know my way around,' he said, as if trying to convince himself that there was some order behind the chaos in his office. 'Come back in a few hours. I'll have it ready by then.'

Outside, in the corridor, I bumped into the same official who had met us at the airport. With so many teachers passing through the system I was surprised he recognized me, but he was effusive in his welcome, remembered where he had sent me and invited me to his office for coffee.

Abdel Rahman expressed his concern about the mix up with my salary. I wondered if he was the official apologist for the Ministry, since most of the time he seemed to be saying sorry for something or other. He asked me how I was enjoying teaching in the hottest part of the country and seemed relieved when I told him that, apart from my lack of money, everything was fine.

I was intrigued to find out about my colleagues in other locations. What had happened to our gang of thirty-four teachers who had set off from London six months previously? Four I already knew about, but how many were left now? How many had gone home?

It turned out that a number had indeed departed, some within a few months of arrival. Homesick, disillusioned, fed up with the hardships of living in Sudan and unable to adjust, they had flown back to London. I wondered how many of them had called into the British Consulate for assistance. Had they met the stony-faced official, who had been so rude, their requests for help confirming her poor opinion of the rest of us?

'We have made some decisions,' Abdel Rahman continued. No one would now receive money before they arrived in Khartoum. The four teachers in my original group who had absconded with their pre-departure allowance in Greece had not been the only ones.

Screening procedures and recruitment guidelines would also be tightened. 'We wonder what questions are asked in these interviews in London. We have teachers here without any qualifications and with no interest in teaching.'

Abdel Rahman went on to tell me about the case of Charles Dickens. 'No, not the famous author,' he remarked when I raised my eyebrows, 'but someone who escaped from an institution in England to come and teach here.'

'I had to go to Shendi to meet him. We received a letter from the headmaster saying that Charles was severely disturbed and that he needed to be sent home. When I arrived, he wasn't at school. They told me he had locked himself up at home and that if we knocked on his gate he would chase us away.'

Abdel Rahman shook his head. 'You know, Mr. Chris, we are quite tolerant in this country. When someone says that something is a problem we always think they are exaggerating. There is always a solution to these things, but this case was beyond us. When I went round to the house there was a wooden figure tied to a tree, swinging above the gate. It was a replica of the headmaster of the school that Charles had decided should be hanged.'

Abdel Rahman made a decision there and then to have him sent home. The police had to be called. The consulate had to intervene too. That was when they found out that Charles had escaped from care. 'Maybe he forgot to take his medicine,' Abdel Rahman concluded philosophically.

He was at pains to point out, however, that despite 'a few unfortunate apples,' the exchange scheme would continue. English teachers would still be welcome, at least for a few more years.

'Apart from the incident I just told you about we only had to send one other teacher home. The rest of you have turned out fine.'

He pointed to the large map of Sudan on his wall, the one that he had spread out on a table in front of us six months previously. 'Perhaps it is time for you to think about where you would like to be posted after Dongola,' he said.

A year in a rough part of the country would be considered a good enough reason to offer me a more benign location if I wanted, but I still had four months to complete and was not yet sure if I wanted to return. There was also the vexed issue of my salary.

'Let me see if I get paid first. Then we can discuss another year.'

With an afternoon to spare before returning to the Ministry the next day, I decided to visit the suburb that John had once taken me to. A few months previously I had written him a letter but nothing had come back. Like everyone else, however, I had little faith in the postal system and there was always the possibility he might still be there.

'This isn't the place,' I said to the driver of my taxi when he announced we had arrived.

'Yes it is,' he replied, 'but most of it was knocked down last month.'

It was unrecognizable. A sizeable community of thousands of people had disappeared, with only a few shacks left as a reminder. On the way back to the city the driver explained that evictions had been popular that summer. Several informal settlements scattered around Khartoum and Omdurman had been razed to the ground. The reason? Someone in Government had decided to get rid of an inconvenience.

'Where did the people go?' I asked. 'Thousands of families could not simply vanish into thin air.'

He shrugged his shoulders and laughed ironically. 'Whenever they knock one place down another one appears somewhere else a few weeks later.'

He told me about a new settlement a few miles further out from the city centre . Constructed of the same bits of tin, wood, plastic sheeting and cardboard it was now home to the men, women and children whose dwellings had been levelled as part of the clean up exercise.

'You know why these people don't build their houses out of anything more solid than plastic sheeting and bits of wood?' he asked. I shook my head. 'Because what's the point in building a better home if it gets pulled down whenever someone in authority decides they don't like it. The Government inspectors complain that these settlements are a health hazard but they don't create the conditions for people to want to improve them.'

I remembered John telling me that most of the population in his location came from the south of the country to escape the fighting. With the war at an end, why hadn't they returned? What were they waiting for?

'You don't stop twenty years of fighting and expect everyone to go home. There's nothing left there now. If someone went back to Juba today, they'd have no job and nothing to do. The south is still being neglected.'

As we drove back to Khartoum I wondered what had happened to John. Was he now living in the new settlement, or had he taken the advice of his family to go and work in another country? I had read that most southern Sudanese ended up in Kenya, although they weren't welcome there either, it seemed. They could only find menial jobs that were poorly paid and lived in squatter camps on the outskirts of Nairobi that were little better than what they had left behind.

These reflections put my own troubles and delayed salary into some kind of perspective. If the worst came to the worst I could always fly out and return to the safety and security that characterized the life of the majority of people in the country I came from. The extent of how lucky and fortunate we were had only been brought home to me after I arrived in a part of the world that had so much less.

'I can take you to the new settlement if you want to see your friend,' the driver said, as we pulled up outside the hotel where I was staying. I declined his offer. There was something much more disturbing about urban squalor than the rural poverty I had seen. At least communities there were intact. People looked after each other and had established some kind of safety net that prevented the most vulnerable from falling through the cracks. The urban poor didn't even have that. They were fragmented and isolated, frequently in conflict with each other and subject to the whims of a Government that treated them with suspicion and irritation. Although the chance of bumping into John was negligible I preferred to believe that he had managed to escape and that somewhere, somehow, in another country, he was pursuing his studies.

'Chris McIvor?' a voice shouted from somewhere behind me in the restaurant where I was eating that evening.

'How many people would know me in a place like this?' I asked myself.

I turned round and there, a few yards away, was George. Plumper, well dressed and looking as smug as ever, he was sitting with some friends. I waved and he came over to talk.

'How's life in the hottest part of Sudan?' he asked, in a tone of voice that clearly communicated his expectation that I would be angry, miserable and cheesed off with where I had ended up.

'Couldn't be better,' I enthused and told him about Dongola's wonderful date plantations, the sight of the river at the end of a hot day and the friendliness of the people. I told him about the school where I was teaching 'attended by the most beautiful girls in Sudan', and thanked him for having advised me to go there when I had had so many reservations. I could see him looking puzzled, wondering if I was the same person he had warned not to work anywhere that was more than a stone's throw from Khartoum.

'How's teaching in the capital?' I asked, after exhausting my list of superlatives about Dongola.

George had quit his job as a teacher and had 'moved on.' He was now working for an international charity, managing projects for people in the far west of the country who had suffered another year of drought.

'My skills were wasted as a teacher,' he said. 'Something more important came up.'

I was intrigued but tried to conceal my surprise. What unsuspected skills did George have? What experience could he offer?

A year as a teacher near Khartoum had seemed enough to convince his new employers that he had the capacity for the job. Although George was based in the city he regularly had to visit the area he was responsible for. I had heard that the journey to Nyala, the capital of southern Darfur, could take up to five days. Somehow I couldn't imagine him on the back of a lorry, bumping and jolting over the desert several times a month. How did he travel?

'We charter an aircraft,' he replied.

As he described the work he supervised, several questions remained unanswered in the back of my mind. Wasn't this something the Sudanese could have managed themselves? With such an obvious lack of experience, cultural understanding and language skills shouldn't this programme have been overseen by someone local, who knew the area, the communities and the politics of the country?

There was also the question of his attitudes. George was friendly enough. He had answered our questions about Sudan when we had first met him in London, but his replies were uniformly negative and disparaging. I couldn't remember a positive thing he had had to say about the country and the people he was now 'saving'.

George handed me an impressive looking card with his name and title printed on it and told me that when I finished teaching in Dongola I could always call him up to see if his organization had some work.

'With your experience I think you might be useful.'

A short while later he asked me if I wanted a lift in his car to wherever it was I was going. 'No thanks,' I replied, pointing to my unfinished meal.

I recalled that only a few months previously he had been like the rest of us; catching unreliable taxis, waiting for buses that never arrived, footing it like the locals when nothing else was available. Despite the discomfort, the pushing and shoving, the frequent stops and delays there was a consolation that came from using public transport. We were interacting with people for a start and not staring at them through the windows of an air conditioned vehicle. I believed that this was appreciated too, that part of the friendliness and hospitality was because we shared these hardships for a while.

Wrapped in his cocoon of comfort and privilege George would now be denied that experience. Working for a charity intrigued me but that was something I would prefer to do in the future, when I had more experience, skills, knowledge and understanding. I was content for a while with what I had and was not prepared to trade it just yet for something different.

When I arrived in Khartoum I had found an hotel that was central, close to the bus station and cheap. The rooms were awful, the showers didn't work and free breakfast was a plate of beans slapped in front of you when you appeared in an alcove called the dining room.

The Nile Palace Hotel was also full of disgruntled Egyptians; teachers, doctors, engineers and agriculturalists who had been sent by their Government to help the people of Sudan. The problem was that no one seemed to have been informed about their arrival. They had been drumming their heels in the capital for over a month and were tired, annoyed and confused.

Not one of them wanted to be there. The consolation was that at the end of a three year contract they would be given a sum of money that would allow them to invest in a better life back home. Clearly intrigued by someone from Scotland who wanted to work in the country, they used me as target practice for their poor English and disparaging comments.

'Zees is a terrible blace. Ze Zudanese are no good. Zey are very lazy.'

Somehow, during one of these conversations, we got onto the subject of female circumcision. 'Do you know that Zudanese cut zeyre women down here?' one of them said, pointing to his genitalia and squirming as he did so.

The group was divided as to whether the operation to remove a girl's clitoris made her more aroused when she was a woman or served to dull any possible sexual gratification. No one seemed interested in the issue of whether it was right or not, whether women should have a say in the matter of what happened to them.

'Painful,' I remarked when they described what it involved. 'Why is it practised?'

Religion, history and ignorance were all cited to explain a tradition which was long-standing in Sudan and which had recently prompted the considerable ire of Western feminists and human rights campaigners. It was carried out in certain parts of southern Egypt as well, a confirmation in the minds of some that the closer you got to Africa the more you could expect barbarisms of this sort. I pointed out that it was common within some Arab tribes as well and that many countries in Africa had no such custom.

I had read something about female circumcision, but it was not a subject my Sudanese colleagues had wanted to talk about. Abdel Atif seemed evasive when I asked him about it, pointing out it was not a practice he endorsed and that it gave his country a poor reputation in the eyes of many outsiders.

'The younger generation want nothing to do with it,' he said, 'but it has been such a strong part of our culture that it is not easy to get rid of.'

Abdel Atif mentioned that the government had once banned all such operations, but making it illegal had only driven it underground and back-street surgical procedures had resulted in worse mutilation, infections and more deaths. He didn't think the noise raised in western countries did much good.

'No matter how well meaning these campaigns might be, they are looked upon as interference in our affairs, as if other people want to tell us how to behave. The Sudanese are very proud. I believe the best solution is to find arguments from within our own culture to convince people that it is wrong. Change in these matters can't be imposed from the outside.'

I fought a lost cause with the Egyptians when I raised the subject of Aswan Dam and the consequences for towns such as Wadi Halfa. Electricity was needed for development, they replied, and some things had to be sacrificed. Egypt's agricultural production had rocketed. There was no more flooding from the Nile. Tourism had taken off around the lake that had been formed. What was the problem?

'Because all the sacrifices seem to have taken place on this side of the border,' I replied. 'Do you know that none of the towns in the northern part of this country have electricity from the dam that has ruined the livelihoods of their people?'

'But ze Zudanese wouldn't know what to do wiz electricity if zey had it,' one teacher commented, to considerable applause and cheering from his colleagues.

Part of me was shocked. Wasn't African solidarity, a common border, a shared historical heritage and a common religion supposed to supersede any of the differences between the two peoples? I did not see much evidence of these factors weighing against a deep-seated suspicion among the Egyptians towards the Sudanese.

It was Arab traders in the 13th century who had given Sudan its name. 'Bilad as Sudan', meant 'Land of the Blacks.' For some people in other parts of the continent the words 'black' and 'Africa' seemed enough to proclaim a country as backward, ignorant and inferior to their own.

My poor opinion of the Egyptians, however, relaxed somewhat when an event took place that revealed a warmer, kinder and more generous side to their personalities.

We had been warned about pickpockets in the markets of Khartoum and cautioned not to walk around the capital with valuables at night. According to my guidebook 'Sudan is known to be one of the safest countries on the continent.' That was why when I woke up the following morning to pack

Girls on a date plantation near Dongola.

A Sufi gathering celebrating the anniversary of a famous saint.

A camel being transported across the desert.

Desert ruins near Kerima, Northern Province, Sudan.

Egrets over the Nile, south of Dongola.

A traditional healer in El Geneina.

A farmer on his donkey, somewhere in the Sahara.

Overleaf – *Sand dunes in the Sahara.*

Preparing ground for planting millet near Dongola.

An acacia tree in the desert north of El Geneina.

The gate of a house in Nubia, showing traditional designs.

The tomb of a Sufi sheikh near Dongola.

A week after the rains in El Geneina.

Wreckage of a truck somewhere in the Sahara Desert.

A sunset in northern Nubia on a trip through the Belly of Stones.

A wooden water wheel on a farm near Dongola.

Young boys herding goats in eastern Sudan.

Girls at Dongola Secondary School, northern Sudan, wearing tobes.

A Maselit family near El Geneina.

my bags to return to Dongola I thought I must have misplaced my wallet and passport. The door was still locked from the inside. No one could have got in. But no matter how long I searched my documents and money were nowhere to be found.

'They use very small children to crawl through the bathroom windows,' the hotel proprietor said when he came to the room after I reported what was missing. The window he showed me seemed hardly big enough to admit a cat let alone a small person, but the proprietor was adamant that children could squeeze through easily enough.

'It's happened three times this month already,' he continued, perhaps forgetting that I was case number four and that this information should have been shared with me before I booked a room. He shrugged his shoulders when I asked him why he hadn't said anything or put bars on the windows to prevent it from happening again.

'Mahlesh,' he said, another Sudanese word that was difficult to translate. Officially it meant 'sorry' but when you raised your hands in supplication it also meant, 'but this thing has nothing to do with me.'

'Zees beeble are no good. Zey are zieves and robbers.'

This was the chorus that greeted me when I appeared for breakfast later that morning. Word had gone round the hotel that I was the victim of a theft and the Egyptians were eager to demonstrate that my favourable opinion of the Sudanese was misplaced.

To their credit, they were also concerned. Some of them had organized a collection of money to help me through the next few days. A considerable amount had been raised. Despite my initial refusal and protestations they insisted I take it. 'We are bruzzers aren't we?' one of them said. I was touched by the offer of generosity towards a stranger they had only just met. I also knew they had very little money too, having been stranded in Khartoum for over a month without getting paid.

Money was not my problem at the moment. Later that day, I would collect a bag of Sudanese bank notes which would keep me in comfort for the rest of the year. What worried me most were my lost documents.

'Whatever you do, don't lose your passport in Sudan,' my guidebook warned. 'You don't want to be in this country without proof of your identity.'

The officer I reported to in the police station beside the hotel was friendly enough. 'Your hotel has had numerous thefts in the last month,' he said, when I told him what had happened. 'It's a lot more than three,' he added, when I mentioned what the proprietor had told me. 'Why don't they put bars on the windows?'

He helped me fill out a form that took an hour to complete. He wanted all my details; date of birth, place of birth, schools attended in Scotland, names of my parents, any previous convictions or trouble with the police etc.

'Hey, this guy is working in Dongola,' he shouted to his colleagues in the back room when I told him where I had been posted. This delayed me for another hour as I was plied with questions about the town and the province where many of them came from.

'Of course, if we had Sharia law none of this would have happened,' one of them remarked after hearing about the theft. 'No one would steal your property if they knew we would cut off their hands if we found them.'

Was he joking? Was this an example of Sudanese humour? I didn't think so, judging by the nods of agreement around the table from his colleagues. Despite my irritation at having my things stolen, I thought this punishment was too harsh and said so. The children who crawled through hotel windows could hardly be held responsible for what they were doing. Their families were poor and desperate. '. . . and how can someone reintegrate themselves into society if they have their hands missing?' I asked.

'They should have thought about that before they took something that is not theirs,' the policeman replied, adding that while children would not be punished in this way they should be soundly beaten.

'What was good enough for the Prophet's time is good

enough for our own,' another commented, a remark which officially brought an end to the discussion. Challenging that perception would only label me as anti-Islamic and unappreciative of their religion and I had enough experience to know that when the Koran or Islamic law was invoked, this was a signal to back off.

Armed with my letter from the police confirming I had reported the theft, I walked to the consulate. I had no doubt that I would meet that terrible official again, the woman who had nothing good to say about teachers when I had first registered my presence in the country. She would seize this opportunity, no doubt, to comment on my carelessness when I told her what had happened.

To my relief, however, a smiling, freckled young woman from London was there instead. She was full of commiserations. 'I think you're doing such a wonderful job,' she said, filling out another form that would provide me with a replacement passport in a few days time. 'Keep up the good work.'

Abdel Rahman at the Ministry was also helpful. He would send a message to my school in Dongola, explaining the reasons for my delay. 'At least money will not be a problem,' he said, pointing to a bag I had just received which was stuffed with Sudanese bank notes. 'I think you can afford a better place than the Nile Palace hotel'.

When I said goodbye he reminded me to visit him the next time I was in Khartoum. 'Now that you have been paid we can discuss your next posting.'

Without a passport I was unable to travel beyond the confines of Khartoum and Omdurman, but these cities were big and interesting enough to accommodate my curiosity and I used the few days to explore them more thoroughly.

During one of my walks around town I was handed a leaflet by a small group of men and women who had attracted a crowd at the edge of the park where they had established themselves. These were the Republican Brothers and judging by the heated arguments that were taking place, they were extremely controversial.

'Why not come to hear our leader speak tomorrow?' one of them suggested when I asked him who they were and what they were promoting. 'He can explain our philosophy much better than I can.'

Tariq picked me up from the hotel where I was staying the following day. A teacher himself he had been a member of the movement for several years and had been arrested on several occasions.

'What makes you so unpopular?' I asked, when he told me that several weeks ago a group of them had been beaten up while they were distributing leaflets near one of the mosques in Omdurman after Friday prayers. As we sat in a crowded bus on the way to the meeting, he told me a bit about his movement and why it aroused such extreme emotions.

The Republican Brothers had been formed several years previously by Mahmud Mohammed Taha. A former engineer and teacher he had been one of the founders of the independence movement that had won the country its freedom in the 1950s. He had aroused the ire of more conservative Muslims when he began proposing a radical interpretation of Islam they felt was too far from its original precepts.

He claimed that the Koran had two separate and distinct philosophies. The first was applicable to the time of the prophet and accommodated some of the prevailing beliefs of the time in order not to present too immediate and radical a departure. Then there was another set of texts he believed pointed to a more egalitarian and flexible ideology that would align the religion much more with the modern world. This included full equality of men and women, more emphasis on the responsibility of the individual and less of a role for the Muslim clergy who wielded too much power and influence over the life of believers. He strongly opposed the reintroduction of Sharia law, claiming that while this might have had some validity in the past, contemporary societies had moved to a stage where this was no longer necessary or desirable.

His claims were deemed by many to be heretical since they conflicted with the belief that the Koran had already been 'interpreted', that its teachings were clear on all major issues and that anyone setting themselves up to offer a different understanding elevated themselves to the same level as the prophet. In particular his opposition to Sharia law placed him in the firing line of the increasingly powerful and influential Muslim Brothers, for whom its establishment was a key objective.

'Such is the level of opposition against him,' Tariq concluded, 'that certain members of the religious establishment in Sudan have called on the Government to execute him and have our movement banned.'

A sizable crowd had gathered in the square from which Mahmud Taha delivered his teachings every Friday. To my surprise, the majority of them seemed to be women. Tariq confirmed that this was the case. The Republican Brothers believed that the marginalization of women in Sudanese society was due to a selective interpretation of the religion by a clergy that was almost exclusively male, and who appealed to Islam to justify their own prejudices and attitudes. 'Many of our supporters are professional women, such as teachers and nurses. That makes us even more unpopular among our opponents, who claim that we are undermining the structure of the family and promoting promiscuity.'

I also noticed that the crowd seemed rather jittery and nervous and Tariq explained that this was because there were police and members of the Muslim Brothers among them. Frequently their meetings were disrupted and on several occasions had turned violent.

'Feelings are running high at the moment because calls for banning our movement have increased in recent months. Now we expect trouble at any time.'

There was none of the adulation and wild applause I expected when Mahmud Taha finally appeared. I had imagined a strong, burly, charismatic character full of fire and brimstone and passion, but the small, bespectacled and softly spoken figure in front of us never raised his voice or waved his arms to make a point and his speech reminded me of one of my philosophy classes back home. The crowd was silent throughout, attentive to what he was saying and more interested, it seemed, in understanding his words than being carried away on a wave of emotion. According to Tariq that was how it was among them. Mohammed Taha had never wanted public adoration or to become some kind of hero. He was a teacher. He urged them to listen, to discuss, to ask questions and to argue their points politely and diplomatically. As he spoke, however, there was a muttering among some members of the crowd a few rows from where we were standing.

'This man is a heretic,' someone shouted.

'Why are you preaching against Islam?' another joined in.

When people began to remonstrate with the protestors, saying they should listen to what was being said, the mood turned ugly. A stone was thrown, then another. When several police vehicles appeared, their sirens wailing, everyone scattered in panic.

'Don't worry. This happens frequently,' Tariq shouted, pushing me down a side street and away from all the noise and trouble.

I was frightened by what I had seen but Tariq was calm and reassuring, clearly having experienced this kind of thing on numerous occasions.

Once the square was clear of people everyone would go home, he said. The opponents of the movement would claim a victory. The police would claim they had maintained law and order. A few weeks later the same scenario would be repeated.

We stopped running a few blocks later, at the entrance to a house where several others had gathered. This was the home of their leader and since I had come all this way to hear him speak, I was invited inside for a more personal audience.

I did not expect Mahmud's keen curiosity when I was introduced to him. After I explained who I was and what I was doing in Sudan he asked me many questions about Dongola, my impressions of the country and, most of all, about my teaching.

'Educating girls is very important,' he said. Although it might be difficult to measure the impact of what I was doing in the short term, I should remember the longer term perspective when I became frustrated by the indifference of my pupils.

'Don't worry when they start chatting in class or misbehaving. Years later they will recall what you taught them.'

Over tea and coffee I asked him why there was so much opposition to what he said, why the arrest and beatings of his followers, why the calls for his imprisonment.

I had used the word 'followers', but he was keen to point out that the people who agreed with his teachings were not encouraged to become cultists or blind adherents in any kind of charismatic movement. A group had been set up of which he was the founder, he explained, but all he had done was to remind people that the Koran could be read in other ways than the one interpreted by the religious establishment of the day.

As to why others opposed him, there were several reasons. What he was trying to do was offer an interpretation of Islam that was up to date with modern social developments, but this was not to alter the religion in any fundamental way. When he said there needed to be an end to female circumcision, that women needed to emerge from the restrictions placed on their lives and that Sharia law was irrelevant to the modern era, he believed this was in keeping with the true meaning of the Koran.

'Ideas only frighten people when they believe their own power and influence is threatened.'

During my meeting with him, others had also spoken, including many of the women who were in attendance. His manner of receiving seemed to be to invite opinions, to listen first and then to respond. The same gracious and attentive manner was as evident when he made his speech. A few hours later he excused himself politely, told me I was welcome and that I could return any time I wanted to.

On the bus back to Khartoum Tariq confided that he was worried. The level of violence was increasing as were disruptions to their meetings. Of most concern was the attitude of the government. Previously they had been tolerated and accepted, as evidence of the pluralism that Nimeiri wanted to establish in Sudanese society when he took power. Now that he was increasingly unpopular he had to shore up his flagging reputation by entering alliances and cutting deals with all sorts of movements and parties. The Saudi government was one of his key financial backers and they were strongly opposed to the liberal teachings of groups like the Republican Brothers. A strong, conservative and influential Islamic movement had developed too and how long Nimeiri could resist calls for the imprisonment and execution of their leader was uncertain.

'I hope they leave you alone,' I said as we parted. I had been impressed by what I had seen, the hospitality and welcome I had received, and the talk and discussions I had heard. Most of all, I had been impressed with the calls for religious tolerance and flexibility, as well as the reflective and thoughtful manner they had manifested.

When I read the newspaper the next day, which described the meeting I had attended as a call by the Republican Brothers for a social revolution and blaming them for the violence that occurred, I understood they would not be allowed to continue unopposed for very much longer.

A few years later, in 1985, Mahmud Mohamed Taha was arrested, put on trial and convicted of heresy and spreading false teachings about Islam. In a public gathering attended by hundreds of cheering onlookers in Khartoum he was executed. Many of his followers were imprisoned too and kept in jail for long periods of time. Nimeiri, who had once announced tolerance of religious diversity in the country, had made the move to execute him in order to placate the Muslim Brothers. The religious authorities in Saudi Arabia had also given their blessing. Nimeiri calculated that his decision would win him public approval and financial support and so shore up his declining popularity. A few months after the execution, Sharia law was introduced. Opposed by the Christians in the South it helped plunge the country into another civil war that dragged on for several decades.

9

Becoming a Muslim

Sitting in Khartoum airport for the flight back to London, I realized how much I had changed.

The airport was the same as when I had arrived; noisy, confused, people milling around, no rhyme or reason in the arrival and departure times. When a voice announced that our flight had been delayed several hours due to mechanical problems I muttered Inshallah, shrugged my shoulders, ordered another coffee and returned to the conversation I had been having with other teachers returning home. No complaints. No expressions of irritation. No comments about Sudanese inefficiency. When someone beside me asked when we would finally depart, I replied, 'Whatever happens there is nothing we can do about it.'

At the time I was still unsure if I would be returning to Sudan. I had received a letter from my university in Dublin, informing me that the start of term was only a few months away. Although I had never picked up any of the text books I brought with me, my thesis had been postponed not cancelled. As far as the university was concerned I could recommence my studies later that year.

'Don't worry. The door will be kept open for you,' Abdel Majid informed me when I told him I was unsure about my plans.

Exam results had been good for the classes I taught and the headmaster had urged me to come back. The Ministry had approved an extension of my contract. If I turned up in Dongola when schools reopened in August, I could resume where I left off.

I knew that London would feel strange. One teacher had

warned us about a sense of alienation, a feeling that what you thought was home had turned into something different. He was right.

The cold, stony faces on the buses in the city, the tight-lipped features of the crowds on the streets, the predictability and efficiency of the public services were a shock after the chaos and colour of Sudan. Quieter and less frantic, Dublin felt more familiar, but despite the pleasure of meeting friends and visiting old haunts, that sense of distance still prevailed several weeks after I returned. It wasn't that people were indifferent. They wanted to know how Sudan had been, but it was difficult to convey the reality of the place and overturn the stereotypes that had also been my own before I had travelled.

'No toilets or running water! How terrible for you. How did you manage to cope in the heat? Three days to get to your village! These poor people! It's so good that you're helping them.'

When I tried to explain that behind the hardships and difficulties the Sudanese experienced every day there was a positive side to their lives as well, many of my friends couldn't see what I was talking about. 'No one can be happy amid such poverty.'

The most difficult aspect to communicate was how much I had gained and learned in the time I had been away. Africa was perceived as an unfortunate continent: wars, famines, corruption, flawed projects and victims. That was the only information ever presented when it made the headlines. That meant that teachers like me, aid workers and third world volunteers were there to rescue and save its people. What could Africa possibly offer in return? I told myself not to condemn this ignorance when, not so long before, I had held the same views.

These conversations drained me and left me feeling more isolated than before and in the eyes of my old friends I could see a similar reaction. To them I had changed, had gone to a place where it was difficult for them to follow. Soon it became easier not to talk about Sudan at all.

It was during my visit to Scotland to see my family that I made the decision to return. I was on a train heading north, pondering my future and what I should do. One section of the railway line near Helmsdale turns away from the coast and into the interior of the country, across a large area of moorland called the March of Caithness. The landscape was bleak and empty, the one or two cottages we passed only heightening the sense of desolation.

Telegraph poles ran along the side of the track, loose wires strung between them. The wind had tortured them into the same strange shapes as the poles I had seen beside the railway line from Karima to Wadi Halfa only a few months previously. I had the feeling that all I had to do was open a window, step on to the roof of the carriage and I would be back in Sudan with my new friends around me.

I realized then how much I missed the country, its people and experiences. I had a sense too of unfinished business, of a journey started but not yet completed. There was nothing to keep me in Ireland, or Scotland either. I had given up any idea of returning to study Hegel and Karl Marx, and had written to the University to tell them that I would not be completing my thesis after all. By the time we arrived in Wick, at the end of the line, I had drafted a letter to the Sudanese Embassy announcing my intention to return and requesting a ticket.

My parents were unhappy when I told them of my decision. The year I had been away had been difficult for them. The mail was unreliable and only one of my letters had struggled through. The news about Sudan was not positive either. The newspapers warned of an imminent famine and claimed that the war was about to resume again in the south of the country. I was thinner than usual, having lost weight through repeated bouts of dysentery.

'Another year will finish you off,' my father warned, openly wishing that I would stay.

I was determined to go and continue what I had begun. I told them that they shouldn't always believe what they read in the papers, that where I was teaching was safe and that I was responsible and mature enough to look after myself. The first step toward Africa had been the hardest and having got through one year, the next was bound to be easier.

A few weeks later I was sitting in Heathrow airport again, surrounded by a group of teachers who regaled me with questions about the country. 'What's it like? Is there running water? Are there enough books in the schools? Are people friendly?'

Curious, eager and apprehensive they displayed the same range of emotions I had felt the previous year when my group had interrogated George. I tried not to sound like him though, as if I knew it all, as if I could predict what would happen to them. 'Leave your preconceptions behind,' I said, remembering the best advice I had received myself.

A few months after my return to Dongola I converted to Islam. My meetings with Mahmud Mohammed Taha, my discussions with colleagues at school and in the places I had visited, my reading of Sufi philosophy had intrigued me about the religion in a way I had never expected. No matter how many questions I asked, no matter how much I read I also knew that until I actively took the step into the religion it would remain impenetrable.

It was not an easy decision. Hadn't Islam been used to justify a war against the Christians in the south of the country? What about the recent killings of tourists in Egypt by a group of Islamic militants who claimed they were defending their faith? Wasn't Islam too strident and uncompromising, too harsh for the liberal values I had grown up with and still cherished?

In response, I reminded myself that all religions had their historical aberrations and that it was perfectly possible to separate out the true message of any ideology from what happened in practice. None of the Muslims I had personally met displayed any antagonism towards Christianity or Christians. In fact, they knew a great deal more about our religion than we did about theirs.

I remembered too the keen, intelligent women I had met in Mahmud Taha's house. When they discussed their struggles for equality and changing the social attitudes that continued to marginalize them, they never questioned that it would be outside their religion. In fact they claimed to have found in the Koran a rationale and justification of the freedoms they were looking for.

There was another more personal reason I decided to convert. Kamal was a teacher at school, an earnest man with a genuine interest in the education of the pupils he was responsible for. He had set up a chess club for the girls and knowing that I played, invited me along. I had a tolerable level of competence, enough to teach those who were interested and enough to give Kamal some kind of competition. Soon I became a regular visitor to his house. In return for being beaten, I was provided with supper and the company of his family.

His eldest daughter, Khadija, was a mature twenty. She was not like the women in the other households I had visited. She would sit in on our conversations and openly contribute her views and disagreements if she had any. She played chess with us, beating me frequently, and would insist that she share the supper she had helped prepare rather than sit in the kitchen with the other women.

'Since I made it why shouldn't I?' she would say to her father.

Despite the shawl she had draped around her I could see that she was attractive too, with beautiful dark skin and deep brown eyes. Khalid seemed proud of her but slightly intimidated at the same time. He told me she had always had a mind of her own, was bright and intelligent and that he had long since given up telling her what to do. She had finished school and was waiting to go to college in Khartoum the following year.

After a while, I realized that apart from Kamal's hospitality, the principal reason I would eagerly accept an invitation to his house was the prospect it offered of meeting Khadija. I tried to look indifferent and proper, conscious of the fact that I was a guest in their household and that any display of interest on my part would be inappropriate and disrespectful. Clearly, I failed. One day when Kamal was busy in another part of the house, Khadija dropped a note into my bag. 'I can see by the way you look at me you are attracted,' she had written. 'So am I. What shall we do about it?'

As with a lot of sensitive issues, I approached Abdel Majid for advice, but this time I thought it prudent not to disclose my own personal interest in the topic. 'If a Christian wants a relationship with a Muslim woman they have to marry and if they want to marry he has to convert to Islam,' he replied to my question.

I pointed out that one of our Egyptian teachers at school, a woman called Myriam, was married to a Muslim yet continued to practice her Coptic faith. 'Yes, that's acceptable,' Abdel Majid explained, 'but not the other way round. This is because the religion of the father determines the religion of the children. So while a woman can continue to practise her Christian beliefs we won't tolerate a mixed faith relationship unless the man converts.'

'If someone changes their religion because of a desire to marry, won't that be seen as hypocritical?' I probed.

'It depends how seriously they take it. If someone doesn't pray, if they drink alcohol, if they don't fast during Ramadan, then everyone will know that they weren't sincere.'

He eyed me curiously. 'Why are you asking me these questions? Have you found someone you want to marry?'

I laughed, brushing aside the suggestion, not wanting to disclose the personal reasons I was asking these questions. Not for now at least. 'I'm curious, Abdel Majid. That's all,' I said, and changed the subject.

Some doubts continued to surface about the step I needed to make. Although I had developed a cordial enough relationship with the other expatriate teachers in the province, I tried to ensure that I was never dependent on their company. This was not because I didn't like them, but I could see how some other teachers made fewer Sudanese friends and seemed more isolated from the communities they lived in. They found it easier to relate only to people from their own society and this was something I wanted to avoid.

Despite the distance I maintained, however, I was worried that my conversion to Islam would lead to my being rejected or ostracized by my colleagues. I recalled George's previous derision of someone 'who had gone native', and the chorus of disparaging comments among the group he was with. Several of the teachers I knew were scathing about the religion of the country, blaming Islam for everything that was wrong in Sudan. Although I was not dependant on the network of solidarity and support established among our large group of expatriates, I knew I would miss it if it was no longer there.

Paul was one of the teachers in the house we shared. He had replaced Arthur who had failed to make any progress in writing his novel and decided not to return.

'Look Chris, it doesn't matter what we think,' he said, when I asked him how he would react if I became a Muslim. 'Personally, it's not the ideology I would choose but if you convert then I'll respect your decision.'

John, who had returned for another year, echoed this sentiment. He had many Sudanese friends and had nothing against their religion. 'So long as you don't become a zealot and try to force it down our throats, it makes no difference to me.'

I decided to wait however, wanting to be sure this was a step I could really take, not wanting to rush into something I would regret later. 'You must take your time,' Khadija counselled with considerable maturity when I told her that I was thinking about converting, but that I didn't want to take the decision lightly. 'Don't worry. I can wait for you,' she whispered.

Several months later, having answered in my own mind all the reasons for delaying any further, I decided to visit Khalid next door. We had continued the friendship he had begun when he first came round to welcome us into our home. I knew that he was a respected member of the town's Muslim community and felt that he was tolerant, trustworthy and able to give me sound advice. 'So how can I help you?' he asked, as he poured the coffee.

I was nervous and shaky, realizing that the few words I was about to say would constitute a step I could never go back on. I knew they would set in train a process that I would have little control over and even at that late stage part of me still whispered that I needed more time and that I still had some thinking to do. 'I've decided to convert,' I stammered, 'and I want your help.'

Perhaps because of the months of deliberation I was expecting a more surprised reaction, a moment of confusion before I was interrogated further. Instead Khalid merely nodded his head for a few moments before proceeding to inform me that there were several things I needed to do before I could pronounce myself a Muslim.

'Aren't you curious as to why I want to convert?' I asked, having prepared beforehand my answers to all the questions that could possibly be asked of me.

'That's no one's business but your own and God's,' he said. 'Practise your new faith with commitment and no one has the right to question you any further.'

Khalid told me that he was happy to help me in whatever way he could. Firstly I had to learn some passages from the Koran. I also had to learn to pray. It would be better to study Arabic too and familiarize myself with the alphabet that until then had been impenetrable.

'Being able to read the Koran for yourself is very important,' he said, 'since we believe that these are the words of God and not the translation of a message by an intermediary.'

Once I had learnt the texts I would have to go to the mosque on an appointed day and announce in front of the congregation that I had renounced my previous faith and accepted a new one. 'You might not like the resulting attention,' he continued. 'The conversion of a Christian is a big thing in our society. You will become something of a celebrity.'

He asked me whether I had informed my family and suggested that I should. He was curious about what my parents would think, whether they would speak to me again, whether I would be prevented from returning home. I told him that while they might not agree with the things I did, they would respect my decision. I could never imagine a set of circumstances where they might disown me.

'It is different here,' Khalid replied, with an honesty I appreciated. He told me that if his own son were to convert to another religion it would reflect badly on the family, his upbringing and the community of Muslims he would have been viewed as having abandoned.

'I would be expected never to speak to him again and to tell him to leave my house.'

'There is no God but God and Mohammed is his prophet.'

Several weeks later, my apprenticeship under Khalid completed, I stood up in the central mosque in Dongola and recited these words. Part of me was still uncertain. Was I doing the right thing? Had I made a decision I would come to regret? As I stood up amid a large crowd of expectant people to proclaim my new faith I felt that I had boarded a train whose destination I was completely unsure of.

Khalid had been right. Conversion brought with it status and attention. My life was no longer my own, or less my own than it had been. As foreign teachers we were all in the public eye to some extent, but people's curiosity had rarely felt intrusive or uncomfortable. Now it was different.

Strangers would approach me in town to shake my hand, saying they had heard I had converted. On the bus to Kerma to visit some friends I was pointed out at each of the villages on the way by the bus driver. 'He's the one who has become a Muslim,' he would say.

That brought a flurry of handshakes, claps on the shoulder and the inevitable question about what people in the country I came from might say about what I had done. It made me realize how religion in Sudan was as much a public and community issue as a private matter between someone and their God. Would I be an outcast now, people would ask, perhaps imagining what the consequences would be for them if they changed their religion.

I continued to live with my colleagues in the house we shared. Contrary to my initial fears, neither Paul nor John refused to speak to me or treated me differently. A few of the other teachers in the province seemed frosty when I met them, not rude or dismissive but more distant than I remembered. I attributed this to some of the pressures they were under. According to John, many of them were now being approached by their Sudanese colleagues at school and asked to emulate my actions and convert to Islam. 'That's why some of them might be fed up, but don't take it personally.'

A few weeks after my conversion a small delegation from the local mosque where I regularly prayed came round to see me. They suggested that it might be better for me to move out of the house where I was staying. It would be easier for me to concentrate on my new faith and learn more about the religion in an environment where Islam was regularly practised. Some teachers at school had made a space for me in their house. I would be welcome to join them.

I thought about this for a while. I knew that John and Paul would not have been offended and would not have taken this as a sign of any antagonism on my part towards them. I accepted too that following the rituals of the religion would be easier if I was surrounded by people practising their faith, that I might well learn more if I was in this kind of environment.

I also realized, however, that I enjoyed the privacy of the place where I presently lived, and welcomed the anonymity when I entered my home and closed the gates. Constant public scrutiny had left me feeling I had no space of my own. My only refuge from all this attention was this house, where I was under no pressure from anyone but myself and my conscience.

'I am fine where I am,' I told them, thanking them for their offer and their concern. I also promised, to myself as much as my visitors, that both inside and outside the walls of my house I would practise diligently what I had publicly committed myself to. I was clear that I wanted no one to say, 'This guy wasn't serious when he became a Muslim.'

Each morning without fail I struggled out of bed before sunrise, washed my face, hands and feet in cold water, and on the rug that someone had given me, prostrated myself in the direction of Mecca and said the prescribed prayers. Five times a day I repeated the same routine. On Fridays I would go to the mosque to listen to the sermon. I continued my Arabic lessons and learnt to read the alphabet.

'I'm impressed with your commitment,' John said a few months later and somehow that recognition, from someone who might have cause to be sceptical or antagonistic, was as welcome as the words of encouragement I regularly received from my Muslim friends.

I had converted only a few weeks before Ramadan, the period when Muslims fasted. Would I be able to cope without food and water during the daylight hours of an entire month? It was difficult enough in any environment but in the heat of Sudan what would happen to me if I didn't drink water?

In the end, this turned out to be less difficult than I feared. Khalid had said that the feeling of achievement after each completed day would help me confront the time that remained. He was right. Several times in the privacy of my home I would hold up a glass of water and say to myself, 'Who will know if you drink this? Who will be any the wiser?' But I always put it down, realizing that any temporary relief would not be worth the feeling of disappointment that would inevitably arrive later.

Despite the fasting and deprivations Ramadan had its compensations. Everyone had talked about the heightened sense of community this period brought with it. At the end of each day rich and poor alike would share common meals. Beggars were welcomed into the homes of the wealthy. Not a day passed without an invitation from a neighbour, friend or stranger to come round and share the food they had prepared.

I had expected too that, during this period, tempers would be frayed, that countless arguments would take place, but common hardship brings people closer together and in general the atmosphere in town was more cordial than strained. Ramadan ended when the new moon appeared in the night sky and the radio in Khartoum announced that it was over. As the community indulged in several days of celebrations, I knew that people were relieved that the fasting had come to an end. I felt I could sense some sadness too, a regret that normal routines would resume and that everyone would have to

return to the lives they had shelved only a few weeks previously.

One day Khalid informed me that the head of his religious
order wanted to meet me. He was a 'Sharif', someone who
claimed descent from the prophet Mohammed. That status
made him revered throughout the town and province. There
was a gathering of his group later that week, and since I had
once expressed some interest in finding out more about them
he had invited me along.

Apart from what I had read in books, my previous encounter with the Sufis had taken place in Omdurman when I
first arrived in the country. On a hot, dusty afternoon John
and I had picked our way through a cemetery at the edge of the
city towards the mosque where the event was to take place.
Even at a distance we could hear the noise, the drumming and
chanting, the background hum that indicated a large number
of people.

The graveyard provided an atmospheric backdrop to the
scene we finally encountered. In the centre of a large circle, the
crowd kept back by an invisible line, a group of about fifty
men presided over the gathering. They were dressed in robes
made up of a patchwork of bright colours and were carrying
green and red flags to wave above their heads. Several carried
swords. One man wielded a whip that snapped above our
heads as we pushed forward to better see what was happening.
On one side there was a small group of musicians, orchestrating everyone's movements with drums, cymbals and chants of
'Allahu Akbar' – 'God is great.'

As the sun descended into the desert the music became more
frantic and the men in robes increased their pace. Some of
them began to whirl around, their movements throwing
clouds of dust into the air that made breathing difficult.
Besides us were some men in wheelchairs who had been caught
up in all the excitement. As best they could they danced
around too, whirling inside the space they had created around
themselves as their friends urged them on.

It was impossible not to be moved at the spectacle, but there was something frightening too in the abandonment and near hysteria. It contradicted the image I then had of a cold, reserved and austere religion and reminded me of those prayer meetings in the southern United States, where conservative businessmen and public figures tremble and confess their sins in front of hundred of strangers. The whole event ended in a kind of cathartic exhaustion. The entire crowd followed the Sufis when they dropped to their knees, touched their foreheads to the ground and uttered a final prayer in the direction of Mecca.

The memory of that afternoon stayed with me for some time. When Khalid asked me to attend the meeting of his own Sufi order later that week, I wondered if it would be a similar kind of gathering. Would I be expected to lose myself in some kind of hypnotic trance generated by their dancing and drumming? Would this turn into some kind of test of my religious conviction?

It turned out to be a much more sedate and tempered affair than I had imagined. The most fevered celebration I witnessed was when a few men began to rock back and forth on their heels while someone tapped out a rhythm on a drum. A few minutes later they sat down to resume their conversations with the people beside them.

Khalid introduced me to some of his friends and went off to converse with others. The person sitting beside me, described by Khalid as a prominent merchant in Dongola, asked me what I thought of their meeting.

'It's a bit more restrained than I thought it would be,' I confided. 'Will the real thing start when your Sheikh appears?'

'It depends on what's appropriate,' the merchant replied. 'Sometimes the Sheikh prefers a quiet meeting and at other times we are encouraged to get more excited.'

When several bowls of dates were passed around we ended up talking about the harvest that had just taken place, the prices they would fetch on the market and the merits of the different varieties the province exported all over the country. Friendly, talkative and extremely knowledgeable about dates I wondered if the man beside me was slightly bored too, the event not having lived up to our expectations of what was supposed to happen.

'So your leader didn't turn up to the meeting?' I said to Khalid when we left for home a few hours later.

He laughed. 'Who do you think you have been talking too all night? The merchant you were sitting beside is our Sharif. He told me you displayed a keen interest in dates but that you weren't too impressed with our get-together.'

I was embarrassed and concerned about the remarks I had made. No doubt I had given the impression of someone eager for a spectacle, but Khalid placed a friendly hand on my shoulder and told me not to worry. Maybe I had learned something not only about the Sufis that evening but also about myself. If that was the case then the experience had not been wasted.

The feeling that I had boarded a train whose destination I was unsure of increased as the months passed. It had been building for some time, a sense that every day a part of me was being lost, that I was disappearing under a set of expectations that were difficult to live up to. It crystallized around my relationship with Khadija and the parameters set around our 'affair' by the society we were in. I never questioned that the rituals surrounding marriage were something I could or should ignore, but more than any other thing they left me feeling that I was a square peg trying to fit into a round hole.

I had spoken to Kamal about my feelings for his daughter. He had guessed that 'something was going on', joking that if he had been beaten at chess as many times as I had he would have stopped playing long ago.

If it was our desire to get married, he said, he would not stand in our way now that I had converted, but during the period before that, we could not meet on our own, we would have to be chaperoned at all times, we could not touch or kiss and we had to observe the proprieties governing the courtship of men and women in Dongola.

I was not prepared for the formality that now crept into the relationship. Once our announcement was made about our interest in each other, we seemed to lose the easy familiarity we had enjoyed before. In front of aunts, uncles, older cousins and grandparents we found it difficult to exchange anything more than a few trite comments, stumbling over words and phrases when previously we had been more relaxed and at ease.

Although Khadija was as beautiful and alluring as she had always been, she was like a delicate ornament I could only observe from afar. I said to myself that all this would change, that once we were married this sense of distance would disappear. 'But how do you know that it will be any different?' a voice inside me asked. 'How can you be sure, if you have had no chance to find out if this is the woman you want to spend the rest of your life with?'

It came to me one day after another awkward encounter that I had to make a decision that would not affect me alone but would also have repercussions on the happiness of others; Khadija, her family, the children we might have, my own parents. With no opportunity to become really familiar with each other beforehand I knew too little to be sure I was making the right choice. Would Khadija be strong enough to cope with the pressures of living in another society, away from her family and friends? Would she be resentful if I took her away from what was familiar, from the world that was all she had ever known?

There was another issue I was concerned about. Although I was attracted to Khadija how could I be sure that we were sexually compatible, that we were physically meant for each other. The closest contact we had had was a short kiss one evening when Kamal left the room for a few minutes, and that was hardly enough to measure anything, for us to find out how close we might become.

With her relatives in attendance I did not want to ask her whether she had been circumcised. With such a high incidence in northern Sudan I guessed that she was, but felt too awkward to ask her how this might affect her enjoyment of sex.

'They're not meant to enjoy it,' one of my Sudanese friends had said one evening, when somehow this subject had come up. 'Sex for women is about having children,' and this seemed to be a prevalent belief judging by the nods from the other men who were there. What it came down to was that I was about to make a commitment to someone I really knew very little about and of whom I would discover not much more until we got married.

'You can always get divorced,' Abdel Majid suggested when I told him one day about my concerns. It was a relatively easy process and a common one, he said. A pronouncement of divorce four times in front of a Muslim cleric was enough to dissolve the marriage. It was as easy as that.

Was it? Really? He acknowledged that women who were divorced would find it difficult to get married again. Their children would be taken away from them, since in Islamic practice custody usually went to the father unless he ceded this right. Without a means of subsistence, divorced women would usually return in disgrace to the household of their family, blame usually falling on them for the failure of the marriage. The shame associated with such a step led many women to tolerate abuse and the infidelity of their husbands.

Leaving someone to that kind of future hardly seemed an option for me. The convenience of Sudanese divorce laws could not reduce the trepidation I felt about our next step.

'I can see something is wrong,' Khadija whispered one evening when we were together and her grandmother had fallen asleep. 'Don't you like me anymore?'

'It's not that I do or don't like you, Khadija,' I replied, 'but I have no space to find out who you really are and what emotions I might have for you. It's as if I am marrying a family rather than an individual.'

In the end marriage proved a step too far. I had become a Muslim. I prayed, fasted and regularly went to the mosque. I didn't drink or smoke, but enough of me had been handed over and soon I would have nothing left of myself or my own values. I understood that I would probably become resentful and angry. This feeling would poison the relationship with the person who had encouraged me on this course of action in the first place.

As best I could, I explained to Khadija and Kamal one evening why I could not marry her. I told them that this was no reflection on her character, and I had no bad opinion of the person whom I guessed was behind the one I, only too superficially, knew. I could not make the decision that would be the most important in my life without knowing more. Since custom and tradition did not permit this in Sudanese society I could not continue any further along this road. I was sorry for any pain I had caused but I had made my decision.

Khadija burst into tears, her disappointment evident. Kamal was gracious after she left the room, reassuring me that it was better I was honest about my feelings and my reservations. He did not want Khadija to be hurt and if I was unsure about spending my life with her then it was indeed better for all concerned to call it off now.

'Of course,' he added, with considerable sorrow in his voice, 'you are no longer welcome in my house. The pain this would cause my daughter would be too much.'

As I left, it was not just the door of his house that shut behind me. I felt that a chapter in my life had also closed. I had made good friends in Dongola. It had formed the backdrop for relationships and experiences I would always value, but I felt that my decision not to marry Khadija was also a reflection of my attitude to a place that in some ways had become restrictive. It was time to move on.

The end of the school year was only a few months away. I sent a letter to Abdel Rahman in Khartoum, asking for a meeting to discuss a new posting elsewhere in the country. After a tearful farewell to colleagues at school, to the girls in the classes I taught, to my neighbours and friends who wished me well, I wrote a final note to Khadija. It repeated what I had said and tried to put into words some of the mixed feelings I had about leaving her. I gave it to Kamal, explaining what I had written and telling him that it was up to him whether he handed it over or not. He thanked me and said that he would think about it. Khadija was still upset but was getting on with planning her life and moving to

Khartoum to study. Maybe a letter from me would not be the right thing just now.

'You will leave good memories behind you,' he said, with a warmth that touched me. 'No one in my family blames you for the decision you have made.'

10

Arrival in Darfur

'Somewhere remote and interesting,' I said to Abdel Rahman when he asked me if I had any preferences about where I wanted to be posted for another year. We were standing in front of the tattered map that hung on his wall, as he ran through the list of provinces and towns where teachers were required.

'We can't get anyone to go here,' he said, tracing a line with his finger all the way to the far west of the country until it rested on a small dot called El Geneina on the border with Chad. I could see he was about to launch into a presentation of its merits; what it was famous for, why I should go there, the same one he had made about other locations he had suggested.

'Don't worry,' I said, already intrigued by the furthest away point in the country from Khartoum. 'I'll take it. When can I go?'

To get there I had to find a truck to take me to El Fasher, the capital of northern Darfur. There were Sudan Air flights, but with inevitable delays, cancellations and the recent ditching of one of its aircraft in the Nile near Omdurman I decided to opt for discomfort rather than uncertainty. There were no lines on the map to delude me into thinking this time that the ride would be anything but bumpy, but I was not prepared for the four days the journey eventually took.

By the end of Day Two all movement had become a blur. Each hour merged into the next as we ploughed through sand that kept us digging and scrambling at regular intervals to get our wheels free. When the heat of the day became too unbearable we would stop, find some shade under the truck and rest for a few hours before resuming in the evening.

At night the landscape picked out by our headlights seemed hallucinatory, a backdrop of shifting shapes and shadows that Hamid, our driver, somehow managed to negotiate. Along a route that was nothing more than the tracks left by previous vehicles, I worried about breaking down, about never being found again.

The previous year a truck had lost its way. The people on board had perished, their dried, desiccated bodies discovered many months later. To reassure me Hassan said that he had been lost only once along this route. The faint illumination of the headlights of another vehicle many miles away was what had saved him.

Occasionally we would bump into a village. Rarely more than a few houses scattered around a well and a clump of trees, we would be greeted by people whose eager curiosity indicated they had not been visited for some time. Over tea and a meal of goat meat and beans we were interrogated about the latest news from the capital; what the President was up to, the status of the peace with the south, the cargo plane that had missed the runway in Khartoum and landed in the river, and the football match that had recently taken place between Sudan and Liverpool Football Club.

Yes, Liverpool. The one and only time I had ever seen a top flight football match was in Khartoum National Stadium on a hot August afternoon when the most famous club in English soccer made a visit to the country and donated the proceeds to local charities. When Kenny Dalglish was presented to an audience of thousands, the stadium erupted in wild cheering. Even when he scored a goal against the national side no one seemed to mind, more preoccupied with his ball skills and reputation than the result of the game.

When the president stood up at the end to thank the visitors for honouring his country, the audience turned quiet and resentful, their frosty silence in contrast to the welcome they had given a group of strangers. The newspapers tried to gloss over it the next day, reminding everyone that it was at

Nimeiri's request that the most famous club in the world had come to their country in the first place, but no one was fooled. The response of the crowd was a reminder of his unpopularity among the same population that had once welcomed him to power. Despite the threat of imprisonment, people had not stopped defacing his bank notes. 'He will do anything to win support,' was the talk around town, and the introduction of Sharia law or a close alignment with Muslim radicals was the most expected option.

With still some distance to go to El Fasher, our lorry ground to a halt with a crunch of gears that was different from the usual bangs and noises I had become familiar with. After a few minutes, Hassan emerged from beneath the truck to announce, in the only word of English he seemed to know, that the drive shaft was 'buggered', an expression he must have picked up from foreigners he had previously transported across the desert. It meant that we were going nowhere until he found another one.

Thankfully we had passed through a village a few miles back. We would have to return on foot, wait for the next vehicle that happened to pass by and hope it had space to transport us onwards. Under a clump of trees in the village square we were scrutinized by a group of children who had been let out of school just to observe us.

'When do you except another truck through here?' I asked one of the older boys.

'Maybe today. Maybe tomorrow. Maybe next week,' he replied, and before he could say it, I added the inevitable 'Inshallah'.

But our luck was in. Late afternoon a lorry transporting dates and blankets to El Fasher pulled into the village with space to take us on board. Hamid would stay behind until someone returned with a drive shaft. He seemed reconciled to the possibility of having to wait several weeks.

'I've done it before,' he shrugged. 'This is what it means to be a driver.'

The next day someone pointed to a group of houses in the distance that I could barely distinguish from the dry, parched landscape. 'That's the outskirts of El Fasher,' he said. We would be there within the hour.

It was different from our arrival in Dongola. There was no smell of the river to welcome us, no palm trees or vegetation to indicate an end to the hostile environment we had just traversed. No one came out to greet us either, our passage barely noted as we entered the town, but it was a settlement nonetheless, with electricity, hotels, a change of food and the provincial office I had to report to. After the four days I had just endured I was not about to complain about whatever I found at the end of the road.

The border between Sudan and Chad is a long, straight line on the map that runs for hundreds of miles until it reaches another border with the Central African Republic in the south and Libya in the north. The result of colonial carve ups that took place in the late 19th and early 20th century, when England, France and Egypt squabbled over their respective territories, the line they finally agreed upon followed no natural features whatsoever.

Nor did it respect local history or the ethnic affiliation of the people who would be affected. At El Geneina, where I was headed, it cut through the territory of the Masalit tribe. This left families separated on either side of the border. When relations between the two countries turned sour, it was difficult for them to visit each other. This was the case in the early 1980s when Sudan accused Chad of invading its territory in pursuit of someone who had tried to oust the Chadian President.

A few days after I had presented myself to the Ministry of Education I sat in the front seat of another lorry, this time travelling from El Fasher to El Geneina, with Ken, a teacher I would be accompanying to my new post.

'They say it takes two days to get there but I've never done it in less than three,' he said, pointing out that if I thought El Fasher was remote then El Geneina was even remoter. The vast expanse of land was still not exhausted. It made me wonder how it was possible to maintain effective control of all that territory, and how people as far away from central

Government as those on the periphery could possibly identify themselves as Sudanese.

Ken was an anthropologist and had little interest in teaching. The principal reason he was returning for another year was to study the Masalit tribe, the subject of a thesis he was writing for his University. He contemplated the world from behind a pair of thick spectacles and an abrupt manner that often seemed abrasive. He never let an opportunity pass to grill anyone who might have information that could be useful for his research.

'Do you mind if I write that down?' was the phrase he most frequently used. No one did seem to mind, partly because he was fluent in the local language and their initial surprise was coloured with appreciation that he had taken the time to master it.

Masalit was predominantly spoken in the area around El Geneina, he told me. Though I might get by with Arabic in town, I would have no hope of communicating meaningfully with anyone outside it if I didn't learn the predominant language of the district. He flapped a thick notebook in front of me covered with his writing. This was the dictionary he was compiling. It was still not complete, he said, pointing to a tree and asking the driver what it was called in the local dialect and how best to pronounce it.

Like many people with a singular obsession, Ken had little time for anyone else's story unless it related to his own. He never asked me how I had fared in Dongola for the several years I had been there. 'So you became a Muslim,' was his only comment when he saw me praying with the driver and the other passengers. 'It's no big deal in El Geneina. People will respect you but they won't make a fuss over you either.'

What he lacked in curiosity about others, he made up for in his depth of knowledge about the place. With several days in a cramped cab ahead of us there was plenty of time to find out all I wanted to know.

Much of the history of Darfur, he said, was the story of conflict. There were the struggles between the competing claimants of the territory, including the Ottomans, the French and the English. There was friction between the people of the province and the central Government that they felt was too remote and uninterested in their problems. Most of all there was the conflict between the settled farmers of the area, the indigenous tribes of the Fur, Zaghawa and Masalit, and the Arab nomads who had come later in search of grazing for their animals.

The principal ethnic group was the Fur, who had given their name to the province through which we were travelling. At their mountain home in Jebel Marra, a volcanic range of hills we would pass through later, they had established the Sultanate which had presided over the region for many centuries. At one time the Fur had controlled a sizeable part of Sudan, their wealth generated by the rich agricultural lands they presided over and the tributes received from other tribes in exchange for protection.

One such group was the Masalit, who established their own Sultanate at El Geneina, their historic capital. According to Robert they had a long history of conflict with practically everybody. In the harsh environment that surrounded it, El Geneina was coveted because of its fertility, pasture for animals and water all the year round.

Like the other thirty ethnic groups in Darfur, the Masalit were Muslim. As in other parts of Sudan, Islam had largely been introduced through itinerant religious teachers or 'Faqis', some of whom came from as far away as West Africa. A number of them had stopped off in Darfur on their way to Mecca, since one of the most used pilgrim routes passed through the province. They had left behind them not only a trail of Islamic conversion but descendants as well. That was why many people had West African names.

Whether it was due to their geographical isolation, or whether it was because the form of Islam they had adopted was more tolerant of indigenous beliefs and practices, the Masalit were frequently accused of being superstitious. I would notice that most of them wore amulets and charms. Their houses were decorated with signs to ward off the evil eye and facial scarring was common to protect them against the spirits or jinn that might harm them. More orthodox Muslims believed that such practices were prohibited by their religion, but the Masalit claimed there was nothing in the Koran that said so. The prophet had worn amulets, so why shouldn't they?

The Masalit also brewed millet beer. Although never as potent as Arak, the date wine I had once sampled, its widespread use was also condemned by other Muslims. They claimed that the pronouncements of Islam against alcohol were clear and unequivocal, and on this matter there could be no excuse.

Ken was intrigued by local perceptions of death and mortality. According to his informants, death was not perceived as the result of impersonal factors. Malnutrition, old age, a heart attack or an accident might seem to be the reason why someone had died, but these were regarded as superficial reasons. 'Yes, that man was hit by a car,' someone would say, 'but it was because of what he did to his neighbour last year that it struck him.'

Ken told me of the numerous stalls outside the principal hospital at El Geneina, with a brisk trade in potions and charms. 'Clear evidence of the strength of such beliefs,' he said. 'Medical science can't compete. The most popular remedy involves a scribe writing phrases of the Koran on a wooden board, washing the ink off with water into a cup and asking the patient to drink it. When I pointed out their malaria tablets was the reason they felt better, they just laughed. Didn't I realise that the tablets were only effective because the prayer they had just drunk made them work?'

Another difference I would notice was the position of women in Masalit society. They were anything but reserved and were quite happy, if not eager, to answer Ken's questions. They were shrewd traders too and in many of the markets around El Geneina they owned and ran most of the stalls. Ken claimed there were a larger number of divorces in El Geneina than in other parts of the country. When he asked why this was so the men he interviewed grumbled that local women were more 'troublesome'.

Over and above the indigenous tribes of the province, Darfur had many nomadic groups as well. These were collectively known as 'Abbala' (people who raised camels), and 'Baggara' (people who raised cattle). It was the latter group who had predominantly colonized the province, having spread out from the Nile over several centuries to find pasture for their animals.

One result of the competition for space between nomads and farmers had been the uneasy and volatile nature of their relationship. Agreements would be made about the use of land, but more often than not these would be broken whenever one group thought it advantageous to do so. Ken had been unable to find any pattern to the shifting allegiances that characterized many of these squabbles. Friends of yesterday were enemies of today and would be allies tomorrow, if it suited them.

I would see some of the ethnic tensions for myself in the classroom where I would teach. Arguments would break out at the perception of an insult traded between boys from different backgrounds. 'Don't referee a football match,' Ken warned. 'It's like trying to officiate in a war.'

One element that had worsened the situation in recent years was drought. A prolonged dry spell had affected large parts of Darfur. Although the rains had not failed completely, the falls recorded had been poor, patchy and unreliable. Agricultural production was down. Wells had dried up. Worst of all, the pasture on which the nomadic groups grazed their animals was disappearing from large parts of the territory. In order to survive they had begun to encroach more and more on the lands of the settled farmers, reigniting a traditional wariness if not animosity.

According to Ken these conflicts were becoming more vicious and attempts by traditional leaders to mediate were proving unsuccessful. He described the situation as 'an explosion waiting to happen'. Just before he left on vacation a few months previously, he heard of fighting arising from one of these feuds in a village not far from El Geneina. There was the rumour of a death.

'If the rains don't come this year it can only get worse', he said.

Talk of drought seemed incongruous in the increasingly fertile landscape west of El Fasher. As we approached the mountains of Jebel Marra we saw fields of potatoes, tobacco and wheat. The slopes were heavily wooded too, looking more like a lush tropical forest than the dry scrubland we had been travelling through.

When someone on the back of the lorry thumped the cab to attract our attention I thought we had damaged another drive shaft, but it was to point out a small herd of gazelle that had emerged from some trees in front of us. It was my first sight of wildlife in Africa and I asked if we could stop for a few minutes, but the driver had other ideas. For a few crazy minutes our truck chased after them. One of the passengers had a rifle and wanted to get close enough to shoot our supper.

There was no way our vehicle could ever have caught up, but the passengers in the back encouraged the driver on, cheering and applauding as we bumped and lurched over the landscape. Thankfully the animals disappeared into the forest a few moments later, while our vehicle was still reasonably intact. 'We're lucky,' Ken said. 'Last year another teacher travelling to El Fasher experienced the same thing. The truck he was on broke down completely and he had to walk for half a day to the next village.'

The sense of having moved into a different zone of the continent was heightened by the appearance of the people we passed. They were darker skinned and more flamboyant than the villagers in northern Sudan. The women were dressed in bright, colourful clothes and unlike their more demure counterparts in Dongola they waved eagerly in our direction, urging us to buy the produce they carried on top of their heads.

At one of the villages we stopped to buy some food. As Ken had said, the stalls were presided over by a group of noisy women, who tugged and pulled at our clothes claiming that what their neighbours were selling was not worth looking at. The banter was cordial and friendly. This display of laughter and joking, their open curiosity as to who we were and what we were doing in their country, was something I had rarely witnessed in Dongola, at least in public places outside the home.

We sat down in front of one woman who served us tea and a local porridge made from millet that was common in the area. She was originally from El Geneina and when Ken engaged her in conversation, her neighbours gathered round to witness the spectacle of a white man speaking their language. While they were talking the infant beside her began to cry. As if the presence of two strange men was of no consequence whatsoever she dropped the front of her dress and fastened the child to a plump breast, silencing him immediately.

Instinctively I turned my head away. Wasn't the sight of breasts taboo in Islamic society? Wasn't this something that only her husband should see? She must have noticed my awkwardness because she laughed and shouted something to her friends. A chorus of remarks and giggles erupted among them, which attracted more women from the other stalls to come and see what all the fuss was about.

Ken translated, clearly enjoying my embarrassment. 'She thinks you have never seen a woman's breast before and wants to know if you're interested to see the other one as well.'

'No thanks,' I stuttered, realizing now that I had definitely arrived in a different part of the country. 'Tell her I've had more than enough excitement for one day.'

Mohammed Atif was a small, bespectacled man with an air of restless energy that inclined towards impatience. He was not only the headmaster of the boys' secondary school in El Geneina but a historian of note, a prosperous merchant and a religious figure of some standing.

Originally from El Fasher he had spent most of his adult life in El Geneina, where he had started off as a teacher in the same school he now presided over. He was one of Ken's principal sources of information about the history and culture of the area, although Ken felt at times that his strong personality and opinions coloured his objectivity.

We were seated in the guest area of Mohammed Atif's large house the day after we arrived, eating the meal that had been placed in front of us. As part of the welcome he extended to new teachers, we had been invited to have a chat about the term ahead.

'So tell me something about where you were,' he asked, curious as to my impressions of Dongola. He had visited it when he was a boy and had retained vague memories of the town and its surroundings. I warmed to him, partly because he seemed genuinely interested in what I had to say, in contrast to Ken who yawned whenever I began a conversation with the words, 'When I was in Dongola . . .'

Somehow the subject of my conversion to Islam arose and he told me that he had once befriended another foreigner who had become a Muslim. This was a Frenchman who had lived in El Fasher, and Mohammed Atif said that he had found the pressure of other people's expectations difficult to cope with. Was this similar for me?

I mentioned that I found the public scrutiny and attention intrusive at times, although I realized that it was never malicious or ill intended. I pointed out that religion was a much more private affair in the place I came from. 'So long as you live within the law and respect other people, my society does not care much about what set of beliefs you hold.'

We had arrived at his house while an important looking delegation was in the process of leaving. These were local chiefs and influential members of the community, Ken whispered, as we were being introduced. He had previously told me that Mohammed Atif was often consulted on religious matters. Curious about what these were I asked him about the issues he was asked to give his opinion on.

'It varies. Generally it's about the interpretation of Islamic law and whether the decisions made by a tribal chief or village leader conform to the practices prescribed by the Koran.'

Today had been different, he continued, and the group that had just left his house had brought something unusual. The previous week a row had erupted in a nearby village when someone had stated that an American astronaut had once walked on the moon. Some of the other villagers had objected, saying that such a claim amounted to heresy. It was clear that human beings could never leave the planet and even attempting to rival God in celestial travel was unacceptable. The argument had spread to other villages and he had been asked to give his opinion on the matter.

Ken was feverishly writing in the notebook he carried around with him. I guessed that his chapter on local superstitions had just been provided with another case study. 'What was your advice?' I asked.

'I said that going to the moon was a waste of time, and the money that had been spent would have been better used to help poor people in the country that sent these men all that distance, but despite my personal opinions I also told them it was an established fact. If they or their congregations needed an explanation of how it was done I was happy to send our science teacher to explain the basics of rocket science to them.'

When Ken had finished writing, Mohammed Atif urged him to be generous in whatever judgments he had made. 'You come from a world where television, radio and newspapers keep you regularly informed. In parts of Darfur these things have never arrived. It's not surprising that the claim of someone going to the moon is ridiculous to someone who has never seen an aeroplane let alone a rocket.'

Returning to more pressing matters Mohammed Atif told us that the exam results in English last year had been poor. The provincial education office in El Fasher had told him this would have to improve. Both Ken and I would have to ensure this happened. He confessed it would not be easy. The principal challenge I would face would be to promote interest among the boys in a subject whose relevance they questioned.

'Islam, mathematics, agriculture and Arabic are subjects they understand the value of, but English is something different. Why learn a language that most of them will never use after school? These boys are bored and will exploit you if you let them', he said.

Later that day at a small café in the centre of town,

Mohammed Atif's warning was repeated by some of the other teachers we bumped into. 'Don't be worried about beating the pupils,' one of them said. 'They won't respect your liberal ideas on education.'

While I was happy enough to hear their observations about the school, the town and the province, I had been warned in advance by Ken that none of our colleagues wanted to be in El Geneina. Most of them came from other parts of the country. They complained about everything, he said, and while the boys were certainly not easy to teach they were never as bad as they were made out to be.

'How have you ended up here?' I asked Othman, a teacher from Wad Medani on the opposite side of the country.

'When I was offered a post in El Geneina the Ministry told me I would get a place closer to home in the future. The problem is I only get out of here in three years' time.'

Ken was right. Even in the short time we spent with them, our fellow teachers managed to complain about the boys, about the coffee, about the people in the province, about the rain when it fell and the rain when it didn't, and most of all about the stroke of misfortune that had left them stranded in one of the remotest parts of Sudan.

'You came here by choice?' they gasped in surprise, when I mentioned that I had requested to be stationed in El Geneina.

'What is wrong with you?' they said to both of us, as they discussed among themselves why it was that people from Britain seemed to welcome this kind of punishment.

The girls I had taught in Dongola had chatted among themselves in class. They often ignored their lessons and forgot the grammar and phrases we had endlessly repeated, but they were always polite, respectful and courteous. A raised voice would always silence them.

These boys were different. From the start I could sense that they would test me, that they were determined to push the boundaries of what they could get away with in my classroom. They guessed that like previous expatriates I would be reluctant to refer them to the soldier outside who prowled the premises with a long, wooden stick. Our 'liberal values', as one teacher had put it, meant an opportunity to have some entertainment.

They were shrewd too, and not without a facility in the English they had picked up, despite their indifference to the subject. This ability was focused not on passing exams, learning better grammar or pronouncing their words more clearly but on deriving some amusement at my expense.

'Can someone give me a sentence with the word "ignorant"?' I would ask, having discovered an expression they claimed not to have understood in some text we were reading. Several hands shot up.

'People from Scotland are extremely ignorant,' was the kind of reply I would receive, a remark greeted by considerable mirth among the rest of the boys in the classroom. Clearly their English was good enough to understand such jokes.

I tried to avoid words that might expose me to ridicule. 'Can I have a sentence with the word, "curious"?' I would try, convinced this was harmless enough not to be exploited.

'The teacher asked the boys in his class about the word "curious" . . . because he was too ignorant to know what it meant.'

At least it was English, spoken and understood, I consoled myself. Perhaps it would give me a foundation to work on if only I could discover something to arouse their interest.

Ken's anthropological interrogations seemed to work. Despite the fact that the grammar and spelling of his students had not improved there was never the sound of the raucous laughter from his classroom that emerged from my own, the constant chatter of students wasting their time. But discussing local culture was his specialty and I felt that the boys would have had enough of it by the time they came to me. Just as in Dongola I needed to find something to avoid the headmaster's increasing concern as to what was happening in my classroom and the pressure I was under from other teachers to have my students beaten.

'Find the boys who influence the others,' Mohammed Atif advised me a few weeks later, after I confessed to him I was making slow progress. 'They will probably be the brightest pupils. Get them on your side and the rest will follow like sheep.'

One of my smartest students was Mansur. He was intelligent, sharp and competent in English whenever he decided to take it seriously, but he had surrounded himself with a group of acolytes whom he regularly orchestrated to disrupt my lessons.

The talk I had previously had with him, the note I had written him to say his talents were being wasted had not worked. I would have to try something else. I found out from one of my colleagues that his father was an important and influential merchant in town, widely respected within the community. After a particularly bad day in class, with Mansur orchestrating most of it, I decided to pay him a visit.

Mansur was shocked when I entered the store where he was working that evening and requested to see his father. 'What for?' he stuttered, clearly alarmed.

'That's my business,' I replied, as I was led into a back room.

His father was courteous, polite and instructed Mansur to make us tea. He had considerable business with merchants in Dongola and we found out that a few of them were known to both of us. The pleasantries over I told him that I had come to see him about Mansur. 'He is one of my brightest pupils. You must be proud of having such a smart son.'

He laughed, acknowledging that while his son was indeed smart I had not come all this way to compliment him on his intelligence. 'Has he been misbehaving in class?' Then leaning towards me and speaking in a low voice, so Mansur who had retreated to the front of the store could not hear, he asked if I wanted him beaten.

I was anxious to avoid getting into the same arguments I had with my teaching colleagues every day about the morality or effectiveness of caning pupils. I knew that if I chose the option of corporal punishment I would only gain the resentment of my students, rather than their cooperation. I was keen to establish a relationship with them that was not based on intimidation.

'No, that won't help,' I said. 'What do you want Mansur to do when he leaves school?'

'He'll do what I did,' he replied, and told me that Mansur would inherit his business when he was old enough to accept the responsibility.

'Being a merchant is an honourable profession,' I replied, 'but do you realize that English today is the key to opening up new business opportunities?' I knew that he exported ground-nuts and other local products outside Sudan and asked him what other countries he traded with.

'Kenya and Egypt mostly, but there are people in Khartoum who organize that for us.'

'I bet they get a substantial profit too. If Mansur had good English he could establish these connections himself without having to get others to do it for you.'

I could see he was curious. The prospect of encouraging his son to be more successful might be an argument I could develop.

The box of items he was inspecting contained tobes from India, the brightly coloured scarves that women wore throughout the country. I noticed that the packaging was written in English and asked him if he understood what it meant. He shook his head. 'You see. That's what I'm talking about. Indian traders have to work in English if they want to export their goods. If Mansur's English was good enough you could expand your business with them.'

Mansur had been hovering around the periphery of our conversation, occasionally entering the back room and pre-tending to look for some item that a customer had requested. After some more discussion, his father called him in. I hoped he would not deliver the kind of threats that would prompt his hostility.

'Your teacher has told me you are one of his better pupils but that you're not working hard enough in class,' he said. 'Do not bring any more shame upon yourself and this family by wasting your time. I have told him you will improve your English. See that you do.'

Over the next week the noise in the class substantially

abated. Visits to the homes of a few of the other boys also helped, but were not quite enough. How could I make the lessons more interesting for the pupils, who were bored with grammar, punctuation and the unimaginative materials we had to work with? With the headmaster constantly reminding us about the importance of good results, I knew that the space to work outside the curriculum was limited.

When I heard that the exam text that year was Shakespeare's 'Julius Caesar,' my heart sank. It couldn't be any worse than 'The Importance of Being Earnest,' which I had to teach in Dongola, but a story set in remote times, in a society so historically, geographically and culturally removed from the one we were in was hardly likely to generate the enthusiasm I was looking for.

'Is it true that Shakespeare was really an Arab writer called Sheikh Zubeir?' one of the pupils asked, after I distributed the text. The resulting laughter surely presaged the diversions that were to come, I thought.

'So what's the story about?' another student asked.

I gave a sketchy and simplistic account of the background to Julius Caesar; the treachery of his friends, the revenge exacted upon them, the antagonism between the warring factions and families and their shifting allegiances and loyalties. For the first time in several months the class was attentive and silent.

'You mean the Romans were just like us, fighting with each other all the time?' someone said.

'Why else would this book have been chosen if it hadn't got something to say that was relevant to your lives and circumstances?' I replied, hoping this idea might win their attention.

'So let's start,' someone suggested, eager at last to begin a lesson.

Abdel Rahman asked me a few weeks later what I had done to reduce the noise from my classroom. I pointed to the text book I was carrying and assured him that I had not digressed from the curriculum.

'I introduced them to Sheikh Zubeir,' I replied. 'That is all.'

11

On the desert's edge

Sudanese hospitality was widely appreciated by the teachers I had come out with, the occasional traveller I bumped into, and in the guidebook I carried around with me which claimed it was one of the defining features of the country. I had experienced it myself on numerous occasions. There was no part of Sudan where people hadn't made themselves responsible for my welfare, determined to show me around and make sure I left their community with a positive impression.

Combined with this hospitality, I also found a keen, almost obsessive interest in what I thought about them. Do you like our country? What do you think of our people? How do we compare to the Egyptians? Be honest and tell us what you think! It was as if our individual experience of what we encountered delivered a judgment that was applicable to the entire society. Everyone felt responsible.

One day, I was walking through the streets of El Geneina when I was greeted by a group of noisy children in a way that was less than courteous. They were immediately scolded by a group of adults who frowned on their antics. Did they want their community to have a reputation as a place where visitors were treated badly?

Over the tea I was invited to share with some of them later, I had to reassure them that my positive impressions of the town had not been undermined by the boisterous behaviour of a few children. As I was telling them this I realized there was a nervous anticipation about what I was going to say. 'Sudan Jameel. An Naas kwaiyzeen,' I said. 'Sudan is good. The people are friendly.' I felt that anything critical, no matter how well intended might be taken the wrong way. Such sensitivity made it difficult to be entirely honest, even with close friends and colleagues.

'So what do you think of our town?' The question was posed this time by a young man who sat down one evening beside me in the small café that had become my favourite haunt. Clearly he was well known. The waiter abandoned the other customers to ask him what he would like and the surly owner came over to shake his hand, remonstrating that it was too long since he had seen him. Mohammed, as he introduced himself, assumed an almost weary acceptance of the courtesies extended in his direction. Who was he? Why was he so popular?

I had been asked what I thought of El Geneina so many times before that my answers had become automatic, super-ficial and rehearsed. Rather than nodding his head and look-ing pleased at all the positive things I had to say, Mohammed seemed irritated and motioned me to stop.

'You can be honest,' he said. 'I'm not looking for compli-ments. For example, don't you think the coffee in this place is awful?'

We both laughed. He was right. The coffee was an un-drinkable mixture of chicory, sugar and hot water, but I enjoyed the view of the town, the company that frequented the café and the tea that was more palatable. Despite the bad coffee, I asked him if he would like one, as a gesture of welcome and to show I was interested.

Mohammed turned out to be a close relative of the local Sultan. He threw this comment out without any of the pre-tentiousness I might have expected. 'Don't look so surprised,' he said. 'Our Sultans have always had lots of wives and lots of relatives too. Most people in El Geneina can claim to be connected.'

Mohammed was twenty-five and still deciding about the life he wanted to lead. 'A bit of this and a bit of that,' he replied when I asked him what he did. He was a part-time teacher, owned a store that sold basic goods, drove a taxi around town and for good measure wrote poetry.

In his 'spare time' he smoked, drank alcohol and had several girlfriends. In a conservative Muslim society this kind of behaviour is normally frowned upon.

'You get away with a great deal by being the Sultan's relative,' he replied. 'Besides, a lot goes on here that outsiders know nothing about. Sudanese claim one thing but often do the opposite.'

I looked around. Mohammed had a loud voice and I was worried that his comments might be overhead and provoke someone's anger. He seemed amused by my concern and told me to lighten up. 'Everyone knows I speak my mind. Why should I hide what is common knowledge?'

I was not so naïve as to assume that Sudan was different to my own society when it came to these matters. Even in the more censorious and religiously conservative community of Dongola I was aware that some of my colleagues drank, smoked hashish and had affairs, but such behaviour was always private, discreet and rarely talked about in public. The Sudanese hid their private lives behind closed doors, which was why Mohammed's more open pronouncements on life in El Geneina surprised me.

Some time later he pointed to his watch and announced that it was time for him to go. As we shook hands, agreeing to meet again, he asked me, 'Would you like to meet the old man tomorrow?'

'Meet who?'

'The Sultan, of course.'

I had seen the Sultan from a distance before, during a public gathering to celebrate Sudan's independence. His residence in the centre of town was more like a palace than a house, with several guards stationed outside it who looked as if they meant business. 'Yes, I'd love to meet him,' I replied, wondering at the same time whether Mohammed claimed more for himself than he could actually deliver.

'See you tomorrow at six, then,' he said as he left the café. 'Please be on time. Uncle doesn't like being kept waiting.'

The Sultan of the Masalit looked the part. Dressed in a white robe and impressive head scarf he waved a regal finger towards Mohammed and asked him whether he had been behaving himself. Mohammed was deferential, sitting primly to attention and seeming to have lost some of his bravado and swagger.

'So you're one of the English teachers,' the Sultan said, motioning me to sit beside him. 'Are my people treating you well?'

On the way to his residence Mohammed had told me that the Sultan had fond memories of the British. This was because they had left the Sultanate intact and supported tribal chiefs and headmen to help control the territory they ruled over. At independence things had changed. The chiefs were regarded by some as colonial stooges and several Governments, Nimeiri's included, had begun to strip some of them of their powers.

'Why not abolish local chiefs completely?' I asked.

'Because they still enjoy a lot of support. No one wants to provoke popular anger by removing them completely.'

According to Mohammed the powers that many chiefs retained were becoming increasingly ceremonial. They presided over public functions, attended weddings and funerals and were occasionally asked by the Government for their opinion on some matter or other. In the political arena, however, they were becoming marginalized. Although many still retained the affection of their people, everyone understood that the real authority in their district was the administrator appointed by Khartoum.

The Sultan was both courteous and curious and, unlike Mohammed, quite happy to hear my complimentary remarks about his community. 'Things must have changed dramatically in the last few decades,' I said, hoping to hear him reminisce about the past and what El Geneina had been like in a different era.

When I told him I came from Scotland he told me that he had been to London for the Queen's coronation. He recalled that it was very wet. 'A few days of your weather would be enough to sort out the water problems in our district for several years.'

It was the splendour of the coronation itself that he recalled the most. In his description of guests from different parts of the world, the palace where they were received, the marching bands, the crowds of people waving their flags I realized what a deep impression it had left behind. No matter that he was the chief of his people. Here was someone transported from a dry, dusty desert town in a remote corner of Sudan to a modern metropolis that was then the hub of an empire. He had been treated well but I imagined that the whole visit must have been intimidating too, a display of pomp and power that reminded everyone where their loyalties should lie.

'Now tell me about your school,' he said, interested to find out how I found teaching in El Geneina.

I told him about the initial lack of enthusiasm among the boys for learning English, the visits I had made to some of their parents and how Shakespeare had helped me out. I remarked too on some of the tensions I had witnessed in the classroom, the rivalries there seemed to be between the different ethnic groups.

The Sultan shook his head. 'It is getting worse,' he said. 'Many of the agreements between the Masalit and the Arabs are breaking down. I do not know where this might end up.'

When I asked him why tensions were increasing he told me that the region around El Geneina had never had enough to support competing claims for pasture and agriculture. Agreements had been worked out between nomads and farmers on how best to use the land, but as drought reduced the amount of territory available, arguments were becoming more frequent. Crops were being burnt by nomadic raiding parties and in retaliation camels were being seized or poisoned.

Echoing Ken's bleak forecast he said that if the drought continued, relationships would break down further. 'It was not like this in the past,' he said ruefully, before changing the subject.

Having finished tea, the Sultan indicated that he had another appointment. With a final admonishment to Mohammed to make sure he behaved himself, he thanked me for my visit and said I was welcome to return any time. As he went out he noticed that I was walking with a limp from an injury sustained during one of the football matches at our school.

'Let me give you this,' he said, handing me a stick that had been propped up against the chair beside him. It was an elaborate affair with a carving on the handle and various decorations down the side. I tried to refuse but the Sultan insisted that my injury deserved some compensation.

As we left the house the guards stood to attention. 'I can see he really likes you,' Mohammed said.

'What makes you say that?'

'Because the only stick I ever received was the one he beat me with whenever I did something wrong.'

Several months after I arrived in El Geneina the normal silence that descended over the town by mid evening was broken by the noise of drumming. Each night at the same time, it would resume. This continued for several weeks. I had heard drumming before but it had never been so intense and persistent, often extending into the small hours of the morning when everyone was supposed to be asleep.

'It's the wedding season,' Mohammed said when I asked him what was happening.

'You mean everyone gets married at the same time?'

'Yes. This is the time of year when people have money to marry off their sons and daughters.'

I expressed my surprise when Mohammed described some of the weddings he had recently attended. For communities as impoverished as those in and around El Geneina they seemed lavish and expensive affairs. How could people afford them?

'They can't,' he replied. 'Some families have nothing left after paying all the expenses.'

'So why don't they put on something cheaper?'

'Because the shame of not living up to community expectations is worse than the hardships they suffer later.'

'That's short-sighted,' I replied. 'People should live within their means.'

Mohammed laughed. He had become my guide to El

Geneina and was able to explain aspects of local behaviour I
would never have understood without him.

'There is something about poor people you don't understand,' he said. 'They are very proud. The last thing they want
to do is admit their poverty. Sometimes they will spend the
little money they have on something they can't afford, just to
convince themselves that things aren't so bad.'

The religious and political leaders of the district and the
Sultan himself, had exhorted their people to be more frugal.
Weddings, funerals and other events should be held within the
limits of what they could afford. There was no shame, they
said, in putting on a ceremony that respected their straitened
economic circumstances.

'Has their advice been listened to?'

'Not as far as I can see,' he replied. 'Judging by the weddings
I have attended over the last few days no one has listened. By
the way, I'm going to another one tomorrow. Would you like
to come with me?'

He turned up the next evening well after I had gone to sleep.
I had been convinced he had forgotten his invitation. 'It hasn't
started yet,' he said, prodding me awake when I complained
that it was too late and that the festivities would surely be over.

With the wavering light of my torch to guide us, Mohammed steered a course to a village on the outskirts of town
that was quite some distance away. We arrived over an hour
later, having stumbled around in the wrong direction because
Mohammed couldn't remember the proper route.

The village square had been commandeered. An array of
lights had been strung across a number of wooden poles to
illuminate it, powered by a generator that hummed in the
background. Mohammed was right. The wedding proper had
not yet started even though it was almost midnight.

There was a noisy fuss when we arrived with people shouting
at each other and a few of the younger men looking agitated.
Someone explained that the band had not received their money.
At one point they threatened to pack up their equipment,
announcing to the crowd that the fee they had negotiated
had been reduced and they had decided not to accept it.

'Don't worry,' Mohammed replied, when I said that I doubted if anything would take place and wondered if it was best to make our way back home. 'They are only pretending. Musicians like to build up the atmosphere. You'll see. They'll begin once they think that everyone is desperate enough to hear them.'

Finally, the music started to a cheer from the crowd that had, by now, swollen to several hundred people. Crates of soft drinks appeared from a house nearby and plates of sweets were handed around. There was a smell of meat being cooked somewhere too. The party was about to begin, Mohammed said.

A few men and women stepped into the centre of the square and danced a few tentative steps before retreating to their friends on the periphery. It reminded me of the school dances I had attended back home; the boys on one side of the hall, the girls on the other, and stony faced teachers in between determined to make sure we didn't do anything inappropriate.

I must have looked bored because Mohammed counselled patience. Things would warm up. 'Maybe you need a drink,' he suggested, offering me a bottle of Arak that he had smuggled into the wedding under his jellabiya and which he sipped at regular intervals.

I declined the offer, not only because there was a group of students I recognized in the crowd but because I continued to respect the prohibitions of the religion I had embraced the previous year and did not want to disappoint myself and others by breaking the commitments I had made.

'This is what we have been waiting for,' Mohamed said a few minutes later, pointing to someone who had emerged from a vehicle that had pulled up on the edge of the square. This was the lead singer of the band and he was famous throughout the district. He was one of the reasons why the family had to pay so much money. As he began to croon into the microphone the instruments got louder, the drums became more frantic and the crowd that had barely stirred before became notably more animated.

As I had feared, I was invited to dance. It would be bad

practice for me to refuse, Mohamed said as he pushed me forward. A space was cleared and the crowd retreated to watch my performance. Across the distance of several years, I remembered my spectacular musical failure in Dongola when I had disappointed an audience with my terrible singing. I tried to imitate the gestures and movements of the people I had seen. One young woman was pushed forward by her friends to offer me encouragement and while she twisted in front of me with an athleticism I could only admire, I improvised as best I could.

The crowd was more generous than the one I had encountered before and gave me a warm round of applause for my efforts. To spare me any further embarrassment the lead singer intervened. There was a new dance in the province he wanted to perform and after asking me to step aside he showed everyone how it should be done. By the time I struggled back to my seat, a large group of noisy young women had lined up around him.

Sometime later the bride and groom made an appearance. They shook hands with everyone and thanked us all for coming. After dancing a few steps they retreated indoors where another, more private ceremony would take place. Mohammed had been invited too, but he said that the real action was out here, with the rest of the people. I suspected he had another reason. At the edge of the square where we sat in the semi darkness, he had more privacy to finish off the bottle he was slowly working his way through.

Once the bride and groom disappeared, the music resumed. There was little now of the reserve I had previously witnessed, or the demure shuffling of feet that had greeted us when we arrived. Everyone was dancing, encouraged by the band who had forgotten their grievances about not being paid. Only when the call to prayer from the mosque in town announced the start of the day ahead, did people start to leave.

I had watched for the last few hours as young children, adults and old people participated in a celebration that must have included the entire village. On several occasions the dancing had to be interrupted, to water the ground so that the dust could settle. It was all good natured and pleasant, with none of the arguments that would have characterized a village dance back home when people had too much to drink. I felt there was something almost feverish in the way they abandoned themselves, as if they were snatching at one of the few respites they had from the cares of their world.

Mohammed agreed with my observation. The villagers were not just dancing to celebrate the marriage of Othman and his new wife, he said, leaning on my shoulder as we stumbled home. They were trying to find some relief from the hardships and difficulties of their lives, but such relief was only temporary.

'The mood here today will not be a happy one. People will see that their troubles have not disappeared but only been forgotten for a few hours.'

When I first heard about drought in Darfur I imagined markets empty of food, barren fields with no crops and children with bloated stomachs. Ken told me it was more subtle than that, that the impacts of drought manifested themselves more slowly and in a less obvious manner. In the relatively comfortable bubble of El Geneina it was difficult to imagine that the district was in the state of crisis I had read about in Khartoum. The stores in town had bags of maize for sale, the markets seemed busy enough and the cafés and restaurants carried out a brisk trade. The weddings that I had seen, despite Mohammed's observations about the relative destitution that followed, gave the impression that things were less worrying than I had feared.

Occasionally, there would be a hint of the deteriorating situation. I began to notice that some of my students were becoming increasingly listless and would sometimes fall asleep in class. My admonishments had no effect. One pupil I scolded told me that the last time he had eaten a proper meal was several days previously, that he did not know where his next was coming from, and that he simply did not have the energy to concentrate on my lesson.

The headmaster was concerned. His request to start a programme of school meals had been agreed on in principle by the authorities in El Fasher, but they had no money to support it. There were other districts, they said, in even worse condition and resources were not enough to sustain every school in need. On a few occasions the headmaster invited us to contribute some money to provide food for the boys. We willingly agreed but it was not enough to halt the steady drift of pupils out of school nor the indifference and lethargy that had crept into the classroom.

As I walked around town, I tried to see through the air of normalcy that prevailed, to catch a glimpse of the desperation that must have been lurking behind it. Once again Mohammed turned out to be a perceptive guide. One day when we were visiting the market, he asked me to observe what was for sale.

Apart from the regular produce of sorghum, maize, dates, goats and car parts I noticed that one section had been set aside for a large and somewhat ramshackle collection of second-hand goods. There was household furniture, bicycles, clothes, books and agricultural implements. Was this significant, I asked.

'Yes,' he replied. 'People are selling their property in order to survive. Last year they sold their animals. This year they are selling their personal goods. Next year they will have nothing left to trade. That is when people will go hungry.'

He asked one of the vendors how much it would cost to purchase one of his goats. He indicated a price and Mohammed said that a few months previously it had been considerably more expensive. The price had dropped because there were now many more goats for sale. People were so desperate for grain that they were prepared to accept lower and lower prices for their animals.

'Last year I could buy a bag of maize if I sold one of my goats. This year it will only buy a quarter of that amount.'

Outside the town I also tried to identify what this drought actually looked like. Again it was elusive. El Geneina was an oasis and the territory that surrounded it seemed as parched as it had always been. I could see little difference in the landscape I encountered, when I first arrived.

'What is drought like in a country that is dry at the best of times?' I asked Mohammed.

Some of his family lived in a small village a few hours north of El Geneina. It was a long drive over dusty terrain, the desert broken here and there by clumps of vegetation and trees where some water managed to penetrate the surface. As we drank tea on the veranda of his cousin's house, I noticed a line of women and children moving out of the village with empty buckets and plastic containers. Why were they ignoring the pump that was near to their home? Why did they have to go further than that to find water?

Mohammed explained that a few months previously the well that had served his family for years had dried up. They had dug down as far as they could but it yielded nothing. Now the women and children had to walk several miles to the nearest alternative source to find enough to last them through the day.

'It takes two hours,' he replied, when I asked him how much time this consumed. 'And now they are worried that if the rains don't come this year, that well will dry up too. The only other one they can use is even further away. It would take an entire morning to collect what they needed.'

As the wet season approached, the phrase 'when the rains come' appeared in every conversation around town. The rains would coincide this year with Ramadan and people believed that their fasting might placate the hostile spirits that were angry with them. In the mosques in El Geneina religious leaders exhorted their congregations to observe this period with more conviction than usual. If everyone fasted and prayed, God would be merciful and reward them with a good season.

Mohammed, who admitted that he had never taken Ramadan seriously, said that he had little latitude this time to ignore it. Such was the mood in the community that he did not want to be blamed for prolonging the drought by eating and drinking during the day.

As June got nearer, the heat built up to almost unbearable levels, the humidity exaggerating the high temperatures even

further. People were hopeful. Heat, they said, was a good sign
– the hotter the better. They would point to the sky that was
filling with clouds, telling me that one day these would be dark
with rain and that for several weeks a strong and steady
downpour would envelop the land. 'But when will it come?'
I asked them.

'Soon, if God wills it.'

One morning I was woken by loud peals of thunder, and
lightening that broke in all directions. The air smelt different
too; fresher, cleaner, less stifling than it had been. Then it
poured a rain I had only encountered once before, during my
brief stay in Karima when a storm in the desert behind the
town had flooded us out of our hotel. Curtains of water
drummed on the roof and lay in deep pools. About an hour
later, as if someone had turned off a large tap, it stopped
abruptly. Within a few minutes there was only a dark stain on
the ground to hint at what had happened.

The school was empty that day, none of the students and
teachers bothering to come in. 'They are in their fields,' the
headmaster said when we went to his office, 'and that is where
I am going too. There will be no lessons for the next few days.'

Was this the start we had been waiting for? Had the season
finally begun? People were cautious, wary and reluctant to
tempt fate by saying that it had. They had been disappointed
too many times in the past.

I realized how fragile livelihoods were in El Geneina when
Mohammed explained what had happened one previous year.
'The rain fell heavily for a few days. Government agricultural
officers announced that the season had started. People
ploughed their land and planted all they had. Then the rain
stopped. There was nothing for several weeks. By the time the
real season commenced the farmers had no seeds left to start
over again.'

'So why not wait until they are sure?'

'Because too late is just as bad as too early. Suppose the
rains come and you wait to see if the season has really started.
There might not be enough days of rain left to complete your
crops. The margin of error is only a few days.'

A week after the first shower, the skies opened up again and for almost a month never closed. Each day there would be hours of stifling heat and humidity as the clouds piled up. Then the rain would come for several hours, bringing relief and a cool, refreshing breeze. The water lay in deeper and deeper pools on the ground, as the earth reached its capacity to absorb it. The dust that had been there was now replaced by a rich, dark mud which was soon covered by grass and vegetation and the land around El Geneina became transformed, so much that I could barely recognize the environment I had become familiar with.

As the maize and sorghum began to appear in the fields, the mood around town lightened too, making me realize how tense and stressed people had been, but no one was prepared to relax completely or to yet claim that the season had been a good one.

After a drought, Mohammed told me, pests were always a risk. The older villagers could remember one occasion when after a few dry years the rains had been good and their crops plentiful. A plague of locusts had suddenly descended on the district and devoured almost everything. Only when the grain had been harvested and safely stored in the large clay containers that people built around their homes would anyone be prepared to make a judgment.

In the end, El Geneina and a few other villages collected a reasonable harvest. Unfortunately, this story was not repeated throughout the district. The village I had visited to meet Mohammed's family, for example, had poor rains. Their well was still dry and it looked as if they would have to walk further and further to find the water they needed.

In other parts of Darfur it was the same, good rains for some and poor rains for most. The talk around town when discussing why this was so, was rarely about the weather or the vagaries of the climate. It was about the fact that the villagers who had done badly were being penalized for their negligence, that the people there had not fasted or prayed hard enough.

A few months later, I was walking through the market in town with Mohammed, where he had first shown me how to measure the level of people's desperation. The second hand section of the market was still there, the pile of clothes, shoes, furnishings and other household goods as high as ever. Clearly people had not earned the money from their crops that would allow them to buy back their belongings.

'It is not just about the amount of maize or sorghum we have produced,' Mohammed replied, when I expressed my surprise that people could not purchase what they had previously sold. 'Farmers are complaining about food imports that are depressing prices.'

In effect, they could barely compete with the maize that was coming in from outside the district, including aid. Some farmers were even threatening to abandon food crops completely, saying that in the future they would only grow enough for themselves and their animals, and plant cotton instead.

According to Mohammed there was nothing wrong with delivering food to a hungry population, but it had to be timed so as not to arrive in a district just when local farmers were about to sell their produce. This whole issue was more complex than I had realized. I had imagined that hunger was a consequence of the weather, an act of God we could do nothing about apart from providing relief. Mohammed and other farmers knew more than I did.

'People go hungry not just because of poor rains but because of the actions of others. The weather is often a convenient excuse for problems that arise from human mistakes.'

12

Across the border to Chad

A few weeks before school ended a letter arrived on my desk with the stamp missing, a corner torn and my name and address barely legible. Even though it had taken several months, I marvelled at the fact that it had reached El Geneina at all. It was the first I had received in the year I had been there.

It was from my sister. Fed up with life in Canada she had taken a teaching job in northern Nigeria. 'I guess Sudan's not so far away,' she had written, with a blithe disregard for the size of the continent. 'Why don't you come and visit me for a few days.' It wasn't only the cold weather she was escaping. There was the end of an affair as well and though she never stated as much I guessed she needed a shoulder to cry on.

The Sudan Air office in town was modest. The smiling gentleman behind its only desk strongly advised me to travel overland if I wanted to get to Nigeria. The flights to El Fasher and on to Khartoum were not only booked out for months in advance. Even if I had a ticket there was the risk of being bumped off the passenger list if 'a more important person' decided to travel. There was no direct route from Khartoum to Nigeria either. I would have to fly to London, double back to Nigeria, return to London and then back to Khartoum. These flights combined would have cost me my annual salary.

'Head west,' he said when I asked him what I should do. 'Sooner or later you'll end up in Nigeria.'

Heading west meant travelling through Chad and that was the place I was concerned about. Although news was often patchy and delayed, stories of an escalating civil war were filtering across the border and occasionally a group of refugees would appear in El Geneina at the offices of the United Nations High Commission for Refugees. There they would be screened and registered before being transported to a camp on the edge of town where they were sheltered in large white tents.

I had got to know a few of them. Ken and I had been asked by Suleiman, the Somali representative of the UN, to provide evening classes to divert the children. Curious as to what we would find, we had both obliged.

Most of the refugees were Zaghawa, an ethnic group that, like the Masalit, lived on both sides of the border. It was strange to hear French spoken by people who looked exactly like their cousins in El Geneina. I tried to understand the reasons for the wars that had beset their country but the people I spoke to barely understood themselves.

The Muslim north and Christian south had been in conflict for several years, much like the situation in Sudan. The north had eventually won, assisted by some disgruntled southerners who felt marginalized by the previous Government. The two principal Muslim groups, who had been allies, had fallen out and were now fighting each other. Alliances had been formed with previously defeated factions, each group in the country supporting one side or the other depending on who was perceived to be the likely winner. It was a mess that no one could really figure out. As their leaders squabbled among themselves to control the country, the entire population watched and suffered.

It was not uncommon for members of rival clans to find themselves in the same camp in El Geneina. In neutral territory they would fraternize, share food, be polite and trade anecdotes about the times they had fought each other. Back across the border, one of the camp administrators told me, these friendships would be forgotten. 'If I see that person again,' he said, pointing to someone he had just had coffee with, 'I would shoot first.'

'Why?' I asked.

'Because it's always been like that. No one knows the reasons why any longer. We're expected to fight and so we do.'

Ken was sanguine about the risks posed to a foreigner travelling through Chad. 'These are ethnic conflicts,' he said, 'and since you are a threat to no one you'll be okay.'

Mohammed was more cautious, pointing out that in a society where the rule of law had been absent for so long, everyone and anyone was fair game. 'Best to be prepared,' he advised. 'Let's go and see what my uncle says.'

A few days later, I found myself in front of the Sultan for the second time, sipping tea and explaining my reasons for wanting to make this journey.

At the mention of the word 'Chad', the Sultan had shaken his head. If Sudan seemed chaotic at times then that place was even worse. The war had recently spilled over into his territory and the far north of the district had suffered incursions of Chadian troops chasing their rivals across the border, but he agreed with Ken that a foreigner travelling across the country would probably be left alone. 'Would you like me to write a letter?'

It was written in a grand style and exhorted who ever read it to treat 'a good friend of the Masalit people' in a manner befitting their reputation for hospitality. I was slightly taken aback when he advised me to show it only to someone who was a member of his own ethnic group or who was friendly towards them. There were some clans across the border who were 'unsympathetic' and he did not want his letter to have the opposite result of what was intended.

'So how am I to know who to give it to?' I asked Mohammed as we exited the Sultan's residence.

'You can't. Most of us look the same,' he replied, 'but I think I have a solution.'

Mohammed's solution was to procure as many different letters as possible. If one of them irritated someone, then I could present another that would placate them.

The district administrator of El Geneina was known to be a friend of Hissène Habré, the President of Chad who had recently taken power. Several years previously, when Habré had been in opposition, he had been sheltered in the town under the protection of the Sudanese authorities.

'Sure I can help,' he said, when I explained the reason I was there and my intention to travel overland to Nigeria to visit my sister. But as he handed me the letter I had requested, he repeated the same warning the Sultan had given me. 'Make sure you hand this to the right person. I'd hate to think I landed you in trouble because of what I had written.'

By the end of the week I had collected letters from the UN representative in El Geneina, a teacher in the refugee camp who was the relative of a tribal leader across the border, and a friend of the Sultan's who had connections in eastern Chad. Mohammed was not finished. 'There is one more person we need to see. Let's try the Sheikh.'

The Sheikh he referred to was the head of a Sufi order in El Geneina. He presided over a movement that was said to number thousands. According to Mohammed his reputation for piety and miraculous powers had spread not only throughout the province but to Chad and parts of West Africa as well. A commendation from him would be useful.

I had met him once before, introduced by Mohammed who claimed to be a member of his order. 'He must be very tolerant to accommodate your boozing,' I had quipped at the time, and my friend had replied that this was one of the reasons he liked him.

The Sheikh, unfortunately, was out of town but his deputy listened to our request and said he would speak to him. A few days later we returned and he handed us a letter. Signed by the Sheikh himself, it urged any Muslim who read it to treat me with the kindness and generosity I should expect from their religion.

'Is there anyone I shouldn't show this letter to?' I asked.

'What do you mean?'

I explained that the other letters I had received had all come with a caution from those who had written them. If they fell into the wrong hands they would arouse anger and suspicion rather than the generosity that was asked for.

The deputy seemed irritated. 'Our Sheikh has no enemies. Anyone who reads this note will help you.'

Mohammed concurred. 'The Muslims that fight each other still have their religion in common. This letter will help you most.'

A few days later a car stopped in front of my house, followed by a loud banging at the door. The driver of the vehicle now parked outside pointed to someone in the front seat who wanted to speak to me. Brian was an American who worked for the same UN agency as Suleiman. He was in El Geneina to coordinate the arrival of a new influx of refugees. Suleiman had told him I wanted to travel across Chad to Nigeria and since he was returning to Abeché, the nearest large town across the border, he was here to give me a lift.

'I'm not ready,' I stuttered in surprise, worried that the final decision I had still to make was now being forced upon me.

'That's okay. How long do you need?'

It seemed easier to go with the flow than to confess I hadn't made up my mind. The vehicle looked comfortable. Brian seemed friendly and the UN flag fluttering from the radio antennae looked reassuring. This was an opportunity I couldn't pass up. I replied as decisively as I could. 'Can you come back in a couple of hours?'

Mohammed helped me pack. He fussed around, regularly asking whether I had this and that, checking to make sure that the letters I had received were safely enclosed with my passport and money.

'Is that all you're taking?' he said when we had finished. Everything I thought I needed was packed into a small rucksack that seemed ridiculously modest for such a journey.

There was a sleeping bag, a change of clothes, a towel, some bottles of water, an extra pair of sandals, a small torch, a medicine bag full of water purification tablets and Flagyll. What else did I require? I wanted to look as inconspicuous as possible. The property I was carrying should appear as if it had nothing of value worth taking.

'You're right,' Mohammed said. 'That way you won't stand

out. Pity you couldn't change your skin colour to blend in even more.'

When the vehicle returned to pick me up Mohammed asked me if I really wanted to go. He looked worried, his anxiety reinforcing my own uncertainty as to whether I was making the right decision, but I had made my mind up and didn't want to turn back now.

'I'll pray for you,' he said as he embraced me. Since Mohammed rarely prayed for anyone or anything I was touched by the intercession he was prepared to make on my behalf.

Although it was only a short drive to the actual border post from El Geneina, I had never been there before. With all the talk in town about the refugees who were streaming into Sudan and the concerns expressed that the conflict in Chad would spill over into western Darfur, I expected an elaborate complex of barbed wire, sentry posts, army and police to regulate the movement from one side to the other. Instead all we found were two oil drums painted red and a metal pole barring the road between them.

Two bored soldiers, who looked as if they hadn't seen anyone in days, sauntered over to our vehicle to check our papers. I reached for my passport and letters, preparing for my first test that could end my journey before it had actually begun.

'Don't worry,' Brian said, winding down his window. 'You won't need your documents.' As soon as the soldiers reached us he pointed to the UN symbol on the side of the car. Without bothering to check our papers they pulled the metal pole out of the way, offered us a tired salute as we drove past them and returned to their seats on the side of the road.

'Will the rest of my journey be as easy as this?' I wondered, as we sped along a makeshift track towards the town of Abeché several hundred kilometres away.

Brian was affable and friendly and seemed to enjoy having someone to talk to for the six or so hours it would take us to reach our destination. The previous year he had been a volunteer teacher in a school situated in a poor suburb of N'Djamena, the capital of Chad. At one of the embassy functions he had attended, the head of a UN agency had mentioned that he was looking for someone to head a programme assisting internal refugees.

Unlike John, who was puffed up with his own importance, Brian was surprised when they offered him the job. 'I thought they would have required someone with more qualifications and experience, but I wasn't going to say no.'

Although I had met him only half an hour previously, I was surprised by his candor and openness. Clearly he enjoyed the comfortable house he now lived in, his paid flights home several times a year and the other privileges of his post, but he was shocked too at the lifestyles that characterized the aid fraternity in N'Djamena, and concerned about the ease with which he had slipped into this environment.

'Some of my colleagues never step outside their vehicles when they make a visit outside the capital. Or if they do they only enter another office which might as well be in Rome or New York. It's the locals who do most of the work. And they only get paid a fraction of what we do.'

As he asked me about my experience as a teacher in El Geneina, my travels across Sudan and the people I had met, he seemed wistful too. He had enjoyed teaching but confessed that his previous circle of local friends and acquaintances had largely been exchanged for other aid workers and diplomats when he had started his new job. Now he missed the interaction with them, the sense of belonging that had come from sharing their hardships and difficulties. 'I wish I was joining you,' he said, when I told him that I had no firm plans when we reached Abeché but that I was sure something would turn up.

Brian's nostalgia was coloured with a strong practical streak and as we neared the town he asked his driver, Hussein, to give me some advice as to how best I should proceed. Hussein was doubtful whether I would complete the rest of my journey to N'Djamena in less than a week. The fighting across the country meant that vehicles could only drive in convoys.

On average, these managed no more than fifty miles a day. There were numerous road blocks to be negotiated and delays could take a long time if the soldiers manning them were unhappy with the bribes that were offered.

'You also need to be careful that your Arabic doesn't arouse suspicion,' he said, pointing out that since so few foreigners spoke the language, people might think I was from Libya.

'Is being Libyan a problem?' I asked.

Both Brian and Hussein shook their heads. Hadn't I done any homework? In recent months Libya had entered the conflict on the side of the opposition groups fighting the president.

It seemed that northern Chad was not just the empty desert I had presumed it to be. There were rich deposits of oil and uranium. Part of Gaddafi's grand plan for Libya was to extend his control over a disputed territory called the Aozou strip, where most of the oil and other resources were located. To further his aims he was providing arms and support to the rebels in the north of the country. 'The last thing you want is to run into a Government soldier who thinks you're a Libyan spy,' Hussein said.

Being European didn't seem to offer much protection either. To counter Libya's expansionist intentions the French and Americans had become involved in the conflict too, providing support for the President. None of this, claimed Brian, was out of any sense of altruism or principle. Hissène Habré was widely regarded as a thug with a string of human rights abuses behind him, but oil, uranium and valuable minerals had prompted external involvement. Several countries now supported one side against the other in the hope of winning future favours from the victor.

What this meant for me was that I could no longer hide behind the supposed neutrality of being a foreigner traveller. If I ran into a group of rebels who thought I was French or American I would arouse the same anger as running into Government soldiers who thought I came from Libya.

'You need to be careful,' Hussein warned as we entered the town. 'Act dumb and pretend you don't understand anything,'

was his final advice when I asked him what he thought I
should do.

One of the 'privileges' that Brian could count on was a flight
on a chartered aircraft that would be waiting to take him back
to the capital. He was apologetic about the fact that he could
not invite me on board. His organization had rules and
regulations about these things and he could lose his job if
someone found out.

Handing me his address and insisting that I stay with him
whenever I reached N'Djamena, he wished me the best of luck
and shook hands. As his car sped off to the small airport where
his plane would be waiting I had a moment of panic and
apprehension. Now I was on my own in a country at war. My
previous assertion that 'something will turn up' seemed more
irresponsible than convincing.

The streets of Abeché were full of soldiers. They drove
around in Toyota Land Cruisers, exactly like the one we had
just been travelling in, but theirs had been converted into
miniature tanks, an array of cannons and machine guns
fastened to their sides. Toyotas were the weapons of choice
and not only because of their mobility across the desert. They
were popular because if the army ran out of spare parts they
could raid the warehouses of the aid agencies in town. The
same type of vehicle was also used to deliver charity.

'This war is being fought not only by men but by children
too,' Brian had said when he was sharing his impressions of
the conflict on our drive through eastern Chad. The soldiers
packed inside the vehicles that careened around town looked
menacing, their inscrutability heightened by the scarves that
concealed their faces and the dark glasses that hid their eyes.
On the few occasions when their head gear had been removed
I could see what Brian had meant.

Some of the soldiers looked no older than the boys I taught
in school. 'Let's hope you don't remind them of their former
teachers,' Brian had joked, a remark which I thought was
funny at the time but was less inclined to find amusing
whenever the soldiers stared in my direction.

By the time we arrived in Abeché it was already late afternoon. There would be nothing I could try to organize by way of transport until the following day. Brian had given me the address of a UN agency that might help me. This one was responsible not for transporting refugees but food.

One consequence of the war was that the men and boys who should be planting their fields were fighting instead. Nothing was being grown. With the diversion of resources from the land to the purchase of weapons, the country was going hungry. The international community had responded with shipments of food aid. Now there was a regular flow of vehicles between the capital and Abeché. With some luck I might be able to catch a lift on one of the food trucks that was returning. 'Failing that,' Brian had said, 'I think you will have to return home.'

A grumpy, French proprietor sat behind the desk of the hotel. He warned me there was no running water, that the electricity would be cut off at any time and that the room marked 'Restaurant' behind him had no food to serve. But Brian had said that 'L' Oasis de Sahara' was a safe location and regularly used by aid workers when visiting Abeché. All I needed was a bed and a place to store my luggage.

The proprietor seemed surprised when I registered my employment as 'teacher' and my place of residence as 'El Geneina'. Was I a tourist visiting the country at this most inappropriate time? When I told him I was travelling through Chad to see my sister in Nigeria and that I was hoping for a lift the following day he whistled through his teeth. 'Good luck,' he said. 'You'll need it.'

The room was basic but clean. It was decorated with pictures of the Eiffel Tower and parts of Paris, images that couldn't have offered a sharper contrast to the location we were in. 'Where can I eat?' I asked a short while later, after depositing my bag and deciding I was hungry.

He directed me to a restaurant a few blocks away. It would be best to go as soon as possible. There was a curfew after dark. The soldiers were suspicious of everything and there was no saying how they might react to a stranger walking around town. 'You have about an hour,' he said as I exited the hotel, tapping his watch at the same time to emphasize that I should hurry.

The place was easy enough to find, but I hesitated before entering. A group of soldiers sat at one of the tables and I remembered the advice of the hotel proprietor to 'keep out of their way.' The problem was that this was one of the few places in town that served food. I had no time to look for another. The curfew would kick in soon and the prospect of staring at the walls of my room while my stomach complained was not very appealing either.

Sitting at a table as far away from the soldiers as possible, I asked one of the waiters for a plate of beans and some bread. The other diners seemed jittery, clearly intimidated by the noise from the ten or so men in army fatigues who had taken over the restaurant and had slung their guns in a careless heap behind them.

I remembered Brian's description of the war as a series of chaotic and impromptu skirmishes, with no one in real control of the competing armies. 'Many of the soldiers,' he had said, 'swap sides in the middle of a battle when it is prudent to do so. It would be difficult to describe them as soldiers at all.'

This lack of authority and discipline was the thing that worried me the most. Anyone with a gun who wanted to show off could do so with impunity.

The food was brought promptly. I ate as quickly as I could and in ten minutes was ready to go, but as I was leaving the restaurant one of the soldiers shouted something in my direction. In the silence that followed I knew I could not ignore him. When I turned around he motioned me to come to their table.

I guessed he was little more than eighteen. 'Where are you from?' he asked in poor French.

'England,' I replied, thinking that this would be easier to explain than Scotland.

'Let me see your passport.'

I handed it over, worried that if I displayed any irritation it would only provoke him further. 'Why are you here?' he said, leafing through the pages of my passport. I noticed that it was upside down in his hands.

In my impromptu French I explained the reasons I was there; the letter from my sister, the difficulty of finding a flight to Nigeria, my decision to travel across Chad so I could visit her. As I gave my explanation, I could imagine how it might sound; improbable. They would be wondering why someone would be foolish enough to enter a country at war when an alternative was available.

'Itkallam Arabi?' he asked. 'Do you speak Arabic?' Without thinking I replied that I did and as the soldiers exchanged suspicious glances, I remembered Hussein's warning that this could land me in trouble. I had just made a confession.

For a few minutes they chatted among themselves in a language I did not understand. But I could hear the word Libya repeated several times. I was worried that the mood might turn ugly. I thought of handing over my letters but realizing that some of them could not read, I decided this would only provoke them further.

'There is something wrong with your passport,' the young soldier now said, clearly enjoying the role of interrogator in front of his friends. 'Tell us where you are really from.'

'I'm from England. My passport says so. I am a teacher in Sudan. I am visiting my sister in Nigeria. There is nothing more to say.'

'I don't believe you,' he said. 'Why would someone from England come here at a time like this?'

Perhaps it was time to be more forceful, I thought. Maybe he would back off, if I made him understand I was not to be fooled around with. 'I want to see your commanding officer. I can explain this better to someone in authority.'

As the soldiers exchanged smirks I realised I had committed a blunder. They would see this as an attempt to question their status. Challenged in front of his friends, the youth who was making all the fuss would feel compelled to react.

My heart missed a beat when he stretched behind him to pick up a rifle. When he pointed it towards me and asked me to repeat what I had just said I stuttered an apology. Clearly had made a mistake in not realizing his position. Did he want to see the letters I had with me so I could confirm my story?

While this interrogation had been going on, the restaurant had cleared. Even the waiter who had been harassed by the soldiers earlier had left. Maybe they were all being sensible, I had time to think, but I felt resentful too that I had been so readily abandoned.

I was surprised, however, a few minutes later when the waiter returned. He was accompanied this time by another soldier who wore the same uniform as the men around the table. His arrival caused an instant transformation. They stumbled to their feet and saluted when he approached.

After a discussion in their language and some angry words, my passport and letters were handed back to me. The soldiers picked up their rifles and headed out of the restaurant. Despite their obvious deference to the person who had just arrived, I could see they were irritated too. They had just been deprived of their evening's entertainment. The waiter winked at me to indicate that my ordeal was over, the dangerous bit at least.

'What are you doing in Abeché?' the man he had brought with him now asked. Unlike his colleagues the new officer did not seem antagonistic or unfriendly. He smiled when I told him I was a simple English teacher travelling through Chad and not a Libyan come to spy on his country.

'No spy would be stupid enough to come here with a story like yours. Don't worry. I believe you,' he said. He went on to tell me that I was here illegally since there was nothing in my passport to indicate I had permission to be in his country. 'Where is your visa?'

Unable to produce one I handed over my letters. He read them with interest but said they were not official documents. In order to avoid a similar situation to the one I had just gone through, it would be best to sort this out. The army barracks was nearby and I was to follow him so my status could be regularised.

'Don't worry,' the waiter said as we exited. 'Nothing bad will happen to you now.' I thanked him for having rescued me earlier. I was concerned that the soldiers who had caused all the trouble might return to deal with him later. They had not seemed pleased when they had exited. The younger one who had grilled me looked as if he could hold a grudge.

At the army barracks I was deposited in an office and told to wait. 'Can I have my passport and letters?' I asked, worried about letting them out of my sight.

'We need them to verify your story. You'll get them back later.'

After an hour the officer returned. He told me I was to accompany him to my hotel so I could fetch my bags.

'Am I being sent home?' I was convinced they had now made up their minds to expel me from the country.

He shrugged his shoulders. Someone else was making the decisions and he could not say what would happen to me.

'Count yourself lucky,' the proprietor said when I told him I would not be staying. 'I never thought it was a good idea for you to be travelling across Chad like this. It's better that you go back to Sudan and find another way to visit your sister.'

Back at the barracks I was made to wait again. I had reconciled myself to being repatriated and believed that the further delay was because they were organizing transport to take me to the border. There I would receive a firm admonishment to get an official visa before I even considered returning. Since this would only be possible in the Chadian embassy in Khartoum, I knew that this was the end of my overland adventure. My sister would have to send me the money for a flight to Nigeria if she really wanted to see me.

Several hours later there was a commotion in the office as the soldiers scrambled around, pretending they were busy. When a young man in army uniform entered they all stood to attention. Thinking it was prudent to do so, I stood up too. I did not want to cause any further offence to a noticeably touchy army.

I noticed he was holding my papers in his hand when he came over to speak to me. I was sure he had come to announce my return to El Geneina and to warn me that I should not think of returning until my papers were in order.

Instead he shook me by the hand and asked if I had been properly treated. 'I am very pleased to meet you,' he said.

His manner was relaxed and friendly, which made me wonder what position he occupied for everyone to have acted so jittery before he entered. As if reading my mind he told me he was the army commander of Abeché. 'I wish you had come to see me earlier. I could have saved you all this trouble.'

He went on to say that the district administrator across the border was a personal friend of his. He had just spoken to him by phone to verify my story. Since what I had told them had been confirmed, I would not be sent back home after all.

'Thank you,' I replied. But I was confused now as to why I had been asked to leave my hotel. 'Can you tell me where I will stay? I have just been checked out of my room.'

'Don't worry. The district administrator has asked me to look after you. You'll stay with me.'

He indicated that he had some final business to attend to. If I had the patience to wait a few more minutes he would accompany me to his home. 'Bring him some tea,' he shouted to one of the soldiers hovering around us, before marching off with his entourage in tow.

As we drove to his residence a short while later, Khalid, who had asked me to stop calling him 'sir', handed me my passport and letters. 'By the way,' he said, as I thanked him for returning them to me. 'I wouldn't show the Sultan's letter to anyone around here. He's not that popular in this part of the country.'

13

The hard road to N'Djamena

Khalid was a generous host and made me feel at home. Despite the constant movement of soldiers in and out of his house he found time to talk to me. Not so long before he had been studying at a college outside the country, but when the war broke out he decided to return. Like everyone else in Chad he had experienced his share of fighting but I was surprised by this easy transition from academia one minute to heading up an army the next.

His principal observation on the war was that external interests had transformed the normal rivalry between clans and their leaders into a major civil conflict. One group was supported by the French. The Libyans and Egyptians were involved too. The Sudanese and Americans backed their own factions. Greed and lots of money had now entered a cultural context where certain rules had previously prevailed.

'If two boxers are provided with machine guns then everything changes,' he remarked.

Over breakfast, I asked him whether he thought I should proceed. The events of the previous evening had shaken me and the memory of a gun pointed at my head resurrected all my previous doubts. The fact that my Arabic, that had served me so well in Sudan, now prompted suspicion also left me feeling vulnerable.

I was expecting him to suggest I go home, but instead he told me that he had already spoken to his friend in the United Nations. A convoy of food trucks had arrived in Abeché the previous day. They were scheduled to return to N'Djamena later that week. If I could find a lift he saw no reason why I should abandon my intention of visiting my sister.

He excused himself a short while later. He had to travel to the northern part of the province to inspect his troops who were fighting a recent incursion of rebels. One minute he was having a leisurely breakfast, discussing local culture and fussing over his three young children. The next minute he was dressed in army fatigues and checking his rifle to make sure it was loaded.

'Be careful,' he said, before entering one of the armed vehicles that had come to pick him up. 'I promised the district administrator in El Geneina that no harm would come to you,' a remark which I found ironic in the context of his own departure to a dangerous war zone.

The official in Abeché responsible for organizing food aid had no objection to my cadging a lift in one of his vehicles, but it was not his decision that mattered. The recognized rule was that the drivers had the final say. If they refused there was nothing he could do to insist that they take me.

At the place in town to which I was directed, some fifteen trucks lined up to discharge their loads with a small army of men and boys ferrying sacks into a large warehouse. Covered in white flour they looked comical and sinister at the same time, their every move scrutinized by a group of women and children who had turned up with empty buckets and plastic bags to collect any produce that spilt on the ground. An irate soldier with a long stick kept them at a distance.

I was pointed to a huddle of men in a corner who were drinking tea. These were the drivers I would have to speak to.

I had been warned that Nigerians were difficult. They would never agree to take me, someone had said, unless I offered them money. Othman was the appointed leader. A huge, burly man dressed in an impressive and spotlessly clean Nigerian robe he barely acknowledged my presence when I explained my predicament and asked for his help.

'No. It is too problematic to take you,' he replied when I finished, slurping the tea that had been placed in front of him by one of his assistants.

'Why?' I asked.

'How many reasons do you want?' he replied.

There were checkpoints to be negotiated. How would they explain a strange European to the soldiers who guarded them? Food convoys had been attacked before and people killed. Did I realize there were no hotels or restaurants on the route? I would be hungry, cold at night and unable to sleep on the ground beside them. All I would do was complain and the journey would be stressful enough without them having to babysit me. 'Go back to Sudan and fly to Nigeria.'

Recalling the advice I had received that morning, I offered to pay. 'I have some money,' I said. 'I realize this will cost me.'

But Othman, to my surprise, seemed genuinely offended. He said that it was not about money at all. My safety would be his responsibility. If something bad happened to me it was he who would be held accountable. 'What would your sister say if I delivered a corpse to her in Nigeria?'

'So that is that,' I thought. 'This man is never going to change his mind.'

I remembered, however, Mohammed's confidence in the letters he had procured for me, especially the one from his Sheikh. Although I seriously doubted whether the head of a Sufi order in western Sudan would have any influence over a group of hostile drivers who came from a country several thousand miles away, there was no harm in trying this last option. Even if for no other reason than to convince Mohammed that his faith had been misplaced, I handed his letter over.

'You mean you know the Sheikh personally?' Othman asked, after reading the note I gave him.

'Yes, very well,' I lied. 'He is a very impressive person.'

'That means you are a Muslim,' another driver interjected. I could sense a shift in their mood, some softening of the antagonism I had first encountered. There was some muttering among them in their language and a few minutes later Othman announced they had decided to take me.

I was to travel in the seat beside him, under his direct supervision and do everything he told me and not complain, even if I didn't understand his reasons. I was not to pay any money either. The Sheikh had requested their assistance and it would be wrong to be paid for discharging a religious duty. 'Come back tomorrow when we will be ready to depart.'

'Thank you,' I said, shaking the hands of all the drivers and informing Othman that I would be ready to leave first thing in the morning. As I left them to their tea I whispered an even bigger 'thank you' to Mohammed and his religious leader. His claims had turned out to be true. His letter had opened a door that had seemed firmly closed.

Several days later a convoy of fifteen trucks pulled out of Abeché and headed west to the next town. The delay in our departure had been caused by the absence of any soldiers to travel with us. The rebel offensive was bigger than the authorities had first realized. Khalid's brother, who was my host while he was away, told me that most of the army had gone north to fight them. Without an armed escort we were stranded.

Two soldiers were eventually found, although I doubted whether the young boys who arrived one morning to accompany us really merited the title. My previous run in with the military in Abeché had made me cautious about asking any awkward questions, but Othman had no such reservations.

'How old are you?' he asked when he saw them. When they answered he told them that they should be in school rather than carrying guns that were bigger than them.

The 'soldiers' grinned sheepishly, as if they had just been admonished by a stern parent. In one sense I was relieved to see that we would not be travelling with some trigger happy louts anxious to pick a fight, but their youth and docility worried me too. Would they know what to do if we were ambushed?

Othman chaired a meeting before we left, going through the procedures our convoy was to observe. There was to be a minimum distance of one hundred metres between each truck. That way if one of us hit a mine the vehicles in front or behind would not be damaged. If anyone had a puncture we were all to stop until it was repaired. If a vehicle had a serious breakdown it would simply be abandoned. Negotiations at the checkpoints would be conducted by Othman and a Chadian intermediary travelling with us. If anyone asked us any questions we were to shrug our shoulders and pretend we didn't understand.

Northern Chad was much like northern Darfur, stretches of desert broken by scrub and thorn trees. The route we travelled followed the tracks of other vehicles which had come that way, less defined than in Sudan because of the lower volume of traffic. The principal difference was in the villages. Many of them seemed to have been abandoned. According to one of the soldiers, people had fled into the towns where they could be protected. The army could not garrison all the settlements and that was why there were now so many internal refugees.

One of the larger villages we passed through had not been abandoned but I noticed an indifferent and listless quality in the stares that followed us. It was as if the people were too tired to pay us any attention or display their normal curiosity.

'That's because they are hungry,' Othman remarked.

'But what about the food aid you have delivered?' I remembered the large piles of flour, beans and cooking oil that were stockpiled in the warehouses of Abeché only a short distance away.

Othman shook his head. This was the fifth time he had delivered food aid to this part of the country and he was still seeing hungry people. 'If your village doesn't support the President or the leader who happens to control your territory, then you won't get fed.'

The withholding of food was being used to coerce people into submission.

According to Othman the United Nations had complained to both the Government and the warring factions that aid should not be manipulated in this way, but he was sceptical whether much had changed. From what he could see the food they had transported was either sold, selectively delivered or not handed out at all. On the journey from the capital to Abeché they would often be stopped by hungry villagers begging them to open their containers so they could feed their children. 'We carry sacks of flour with messages that read, 'A gift from the people of the United States.' Do they know what is happening to the food they have sent?'

The town where we would stay overnight was different from the villages we had earlier passed through. It was packed with people for a start and seemed more like the bustling settlements I was familiar with in Sudan. As we entered the dusty outskirts, we drove through a sprawling area of tents and makeshift shelters. This was where the refugees lived, the people from the surrounding country who had abandoned their homes.

Othman was angry. Our soldiers had announced that they were going no further. They would look for a vehicle to take them back to Abéché the following day. 'Why?' I asked, since it had been agreed they would accompany us to N'Djamena.

'They're eager to get shot at so they can tell their families they've been in a war. Escorting trucks is not exciting enough for them.'

As Othman and our Chadian interlocutor marched off to find some other soldiers, I took the opportunity to walk around. The market at the edge of the square was open and I was surprised at the area it covered, the number of people still milling around and the range of goods for sale. At one of the busiest sections of the market I stopped in front of some stalls where sacks of maize and beans and bottles of cooking oil were prominently displayed. Many were marked 'Not For Sale' and looked exactly like the produce that had been offloaded in Abéché a few days previously.

I pointed to the flour that one of the traders was pouring into small plastic bags. Why was he selling food that people were supposed to receive rather than pay for? He seemed surprised by the question and shrugged his shoulders. 'I bought it. Now I am selling it,' he said, and signalled me to move on unless I wanted to buy some.

The drivers were more upbeat when I returned. A deal had been struck with the local army commander and we would have some soldiers the following day so that we could proceed with our journey.

Othman seemed more relaxed too. He had progressively shed the abrasive and offhand manner I encountered when we first met. The fact that I hadn't complained about the bumpy ride, the long hard hours of travel or the heat of the day seemed to have won me some favour. Over the supper we ate later, he told me that this would be his final trip. 'The pay is good but every time my wife and children say goodbye they think I won't be coming home.'

It wasn't just the danger, the long hours and the uncertainty of knowing whether they could travel from one day to the next that upset him. The whimsicality of the authorities angered him too, especially when he could see people suffering. The fact that food aid was being sold in the market to people who should be receiving it free was typical of the self-interest and corruption that prevailed in the country. 'There is no reason why people here should be starving.'

The lights that illuminated the square where our trucks were parked went out later. Electricity was only available for a few hours. Around the fire the drivers chatted and laughed and, for a few moments, it felt as if I was back in Sudan. Though I could not follow what they were saying, I found their conversation reassuring, pushing behind me the worries I had about the next few days.

There were other fires like our own, around which groups of people had collected. Hearing them talk, the noise of their laughter, made it seem as if the fighting and misery were miles away, in a different time and place, but that feeling of being far away did not last long. Some time that evening I woke up to a loud commotion. Othman was tugging at his blanket, a large dog on the end of it pulling in the opposite direction.

Another driver jumped up and threw one of the pieces of still smouldering wood towards it. As the animal jumped away, the shower of sparks illuminated several others prowling around the square. 'Hunger has made these dogs bold,' I thought when the clamour had died down and the fire had been relit.

'Sleep with your head towards the fire,' Othman told me. 'If you need a pee don't go far.'

'But these are only dogs,' I replied. Although they might be hungry they would never attack us. 'They are only after the scraps of food discarded from our meal.'

Tossing another piece of lighted wood in the direction of the animals in the distance he told me to take a good look to see what was there. 'These are hyenas, not dogs,' he said, when I drew back in surprise. 'Don't think they won't attack you. They're as hungry as everyone else in this country and more desperate too.'

For the few hours of darkness that remained, I was unable to sleep. The hyenas continued to circle around our fire, which one of the drivers kept alight by throwing on pieces of wood. Their red eyes and ridiculous cackle frightened me most. It was as if they had taken over the town. More than the people who lived here these animals seemed to be the true owners of this territory. It was we who were the intruders.

Each day was much the same as the previous one. We made slow progress through a desert landscape that was occasionally interrupted by a tired and hungry village. In several of the stores that were open, I saw empty shelves and nothing for sale. 'But we have coca-cola,' one shopkeeper announced. Watched by a crowd of emaciated looking children I did not have the courage, despite my thirst, to buy one.

The soldiers who guarded these settlements were harmless and bored, losing interest when they were informed that our vehicles were empty. The prospect of a bribe removed, they waved us on.

Generally I was left alone, the explanations of our guide enough to quell the occasional suspicion about why a foreigner was travelling through the country but, at one stop, word got round that the follower of a famous Sufi had arrived. Apparently I was available for consultations too. Soon I had a small queue of people in front of me, presenting a variety of ailments I was supposed to cure. 'Give them an aspirin,' Othman advised. 'At least it won't do them any harm.'

That evening, when we met a convoy travelling in the opposite direction, the soldiers we had picked up earlier in the day abandoned us like the previous ones. Othman and our minder marched off again, returning a few hours later looking glum and disgruntled. Although a deal had been struck with the local army commander, it had cost a lot of money. If our soldiers continued to leave us at this rate, Othman's 'bribery fund' would soon be exhausted. The prospect of being stranded in the middle of Chad appealed to no one, but Othman was not only worried about the fickleness of our escort.

'What's up?' I enquired, familiar enough with him now to feel I could ask.

He was concerned about the following day. The territory we would pass through was difficult, an area of sand and steep dunes that would slow our progress. It was also an area that the Government had no control over. There were bandits who regularly attacked convoys like ours. On a previous occasion Othman and his men had lost a truck. As they were digging it out of a sand dune they had heard shots nearby. When a group of men on camels appeared in the distance advancing in their direction, they had driven off as fast as they could, leaving the other vehicle behind.

'Tomorrow will be uncomfortable and dangerous. The best way to get through this place is to drive as hard as we can in the hope we won't get stuck. There will be no stopping until the next town on the other side.'

Placing a hand on my shoulder, Othman asked me if I wanted to continue. 'Unlike us you have a choice. There is no shame in returning home.'

Once again I was tempted. As Othman said, there would be no shame in giving up. I had done the best I could. At the time I received my sister's letter over a month previously I made a decision whose consequences I could not have foreseen. Returning home would be more an act of prudence than cowardice, but it was not as easy as that. The problem was that with each obstacle overcome it became more difficult to pull out. It was as if some voice inside me was saying, 'Look, you have come this far. What a pity to give up now.'

I realised, too, how persistent that voice could be. I imagined myself back in El Geneina, angry that I had not continued and disappointed at turning home before I really had to. The measure I had set myself by coming to Sudan was not about being foolhardy or stupid, but I felt an obligation to try as hard as I could and not shirk the challenges that confronted me.

After some deliberation I said to myself that if Othman was genuinely concerned about my safety, or believed I was in real danger, he would simply have told me he could take me no further. 'It's okay. I'm not ready to give up yet,' I said, thanking him at the same time for the opportunity. 'If something happens I won't blame you.'

From the edge of an escarpment the next morning we could see a vast area of dunes in front of us and a range of hills beyond. The drivers disembarked, said a few prayers and shook hands before returning to their cabs. The mood was sombre and serious. The soldiers travelling with us had told us that a few days previously some trucks travelling through this area had been shot at. People had been killed.

Othman was right. The journey was long and uncomfortable. Whenever we could, we picked up speed so the momentum would push us through the soft sand where we might get stuck. The burnt out shells of several trucks provided a stark reminder of what might happen if we did. There was one nervous halt to repair a puncture and I marvelled at how an operation which had taken an hour to perform on a previous occasion was completed this time in a few brief minutes.

'We are through the worst of it now,' Othman said that afternoon, the town where we were headed just visible on the other side of the dunes. The bandits generally kept away from populated areas. It seemed that we were safe, but Othman was taking no chances.

Despite our weariness he insisted that we continue until we reached the outskirts of the settlement that was still a few hours away. When we finally came to a halt we all stumbled out of the trucks and ran for the nearest clump of trees. 'Pee out of the window,' Othman said earlier, when I had asked him to stop so I could relieve myself.

I was worried that our soldiers would abandon us again, but Othman was more hopeful. One of them had family in N'Djamena and so had good reason to continue all the way. To offer encouragement Othman purchased some goats, announcing to everyone that we would eat well for the rest of the journey. It seemed to work because the soldiers were still there the following morning. Perhaps we would get to N'Djamena after all.

Four days later, a week after I had left Abeché and ten days after I had departed Sudan, I said goodbye to Othman and the other drivers. On the outskirts of a city that seemed much like all the other towns and villages we had passed through; small mud huts, potholed streets, women selling meagre piles of vegetables by the side of the road, I left them at a checkpoint manned by Chadian soldiers. Almost at our journey's end they were demanding an impossible bribe to let us through.

'It's best you go on,' Othman said. 'We could be here for days.' With these words he hugged me warmly, told me I was welcome to visit him in Nigeria any time and said that he would speak to his other compatriots working in 'this wretched country.' If I turned up at the warehouse in N'Djamena from where all the food convoys headed out, I would be assured of a lift whenever I returned.

I took up Brian's offer to stay with him. He lived in a fenced off part of the city, in a small island of smart houses with electricity and running water, roads without holes. It was a suburb that looked as if it had been imported wholesale from another country. The abrupt change to a room with a bed, shower, air conditioning and a television with imported channels took a while to get used to, but part of me enjoyed the contrast too, the feeling that I had earned the right to a few luxuries after a fortnight of difficult travel.

Originally, I had thought my stay in the capital would be no more than a few days. Familiar with how things worked in Chad, Brian warned me not to be over-optimistic.

The Nigerian Embassy was difficult. Why hadn't I procured a visa in Sudan?

'Because I don't work in Khartoum,' was an argument that seemed to convince no one. The person I spoke to was unimpressed too when I described the difficult journey I had just endured, my desire to visit my sister and my plea that if I couldn't proceed this way there was no alternative but to go back without seeing her at all.

'I have to send a letter to our people in Lagos,' a plump Nigerian lady scowled when I pressed her for something more definite than her vague commitment to 'see what I can do.'

'How long will that take?'

'It will take a week maybe, perhaps longer.'

'What am I supposed to do in the meantime?' I asked.

She shrugged her shoulders and picked up the phone to let me know that she had more important things to get on with. 'Come back next week. That's the best I can offer.'

Brian was a good host. He seemed to enjoy my company and took time to show me a city I was curious to see. In many ways it resembled Khartoum. There was a smart business district with office blocks, posh hotels and stores run by foreign traders. There was an area reserved for Ministry buildings and embassies, but like the suburb where Brian lived, these were little islands in a bigger sea of poverty and overcrowding.

Most of N'Djamena was characterized by poor housing, streets with open sewers and piles of uncollected garbage. The roads were barely able to cope with the traffic that crawled along them. The principal difference I noticed from the impoverished villages I had earlier passed through was the forest of radio and television antennas above the roofs of the houses. That was the only luxury people in the city could afford, Brian observed.

Just as in Khartoum these places had a vibrancy and colour that the better off parts of the city lacked. People greeted us when we walked down the streets. The hawkers urging us to buy cheap plastic goods from India engaged us in conversation even when we said we weren't interested. In one of the downtown restaurants where Brian took me, the atmosphere was warm and friendly, unlike the smarter location where we had eaten the previous evening. 'Maybe it's the company that makes the food taste better,' I observed.

A few days later Brian arrived home to announce that we would be doing something different that evening. 'To meet the great and the good,' he replied, when I asked him where we were going.

The US ambassador was hosting a function for the press corps that had recently descended on the capital. International attention was beginning to focus on the conflict in Chad, bringing the media with it. The heads of several aid agencies would be there, explaining how they were helping the country's victims.

The journalists who pitched up were angry and frustrated. The Government had refused them permission to travel outside the city. They had spent the last few weeks in their hotel rooms, trying to make something interesting out of the scant information provided by the authorities. The press statements released by the agencies hadn't helped either.

Several days ago a visit to an area outside the city had been organized by the Ministry of Information, carefully orchestrated to present the Government in the best possible light. Brian said that it had left the press feeling more manipulated than informed. This function was partly designed to placate them.

'Can you honestly say that food aid is getting to the people who need it the most?' The question was directed to an agency spokesman, who had just completed a very slick, professional and inaccurate presentation of what was happening on the ground.

'Yes,' he replied. 'There is no evidence to indicate any interference in our distributions.'

Brian nudged me. I had told him about my journey through the country and what I had seen. In the pause before the next question he whispered to me that I should take this opportunity to speak out. I hesitated. Was this the right occasion and who would believe me? 'Go ahead,' he insisted. 'It's your chance to tell everyone what is happening.'

I stood up and drew a deep breath. 'Excuse me, but I've

travelled across this country for the last few weeks and what you say about food deliveries is untrue.' I related what I had seen and heard: the food kept in warehouses, the bribery and corruption, the hungry people, the selective distributions, the food being sold for a profit by government officials and unscrupulous traders. When I sat down there was complete silence, apart from a scratching of pens on paper among the journalists.

The agency official was defensive. 'A few isolated villages aren't indicative of what is happening in the rest of the country.'

'I saw this in every village I passed through,' I responded. 'And why don't you ask the drivers who transport your food? They'll tell you the same story.'

At the end I was surrounded by a group of journalists wanting more information on what I had seen. Over and above my observations on food aid they were intrigued as to how I had managed to bypass the Government restrictions on travel that had limited their own movements. I described the preparations I had made before my journey, the contacts I had established and how a series of letters from influential people had allowed me to traverse the country.

At home a few hours later I apologized to Brian for any embarrassment I might have caused him in front of his bosses. 'I don't think you'll get invited to any functions again, or at least you'll be told not to bring your friends'. But he was pleased I had stood up and related what I had seen.

'Have you ever thought of writing this down yourself,' he asked, 'instead of letting some journalist get the credit for your story?'

I told him about a letter I had once sent to the Irish Times asking them for a job. The reply when it came conveyed a clear message that I had nothing to offer. Several years of academic study, a degree in philosophy and no previous experience of writing was hardly enough to launch a newspaper career. 'Write back when you have something to say,' the note concluded.

'So why don't you?'

'Because they probably have their own journalist on this story,' I replied.

'You'll never know if you don't try.'

Brian was certainly persistent. He had a fax machine at his office. He would find the address of the Irish Times. If I typed out the story of what I had seen on my journey through Chad, he would send it off as soon as it was ready.

The following day I woke up to find a typewriter on the table, some paper and a note from Brian to say that he expected to read something when he returned. 'No harm in trying,' I thought, attempting several drafts before coming up with something I was happy with.

A few days later Brian returned with the reply. It was from the foreign editor of the Irish Times. He had read my article, liked it and had printed it. He also wanted to know if I had more material. Could I retrace my steps along the route I had come and write a series of articles on what I observed? At the bottom of his note was a request to let him know where he should send the money for the piece that had already been published.

'So this journey has turned you into a scribe,' Brian said, as I read the letter several times.

I thanked him for all his support. Without his encouragement I would never have thought my views were of sufficient interest to be included in the pages of an international newspaper, but part of me felt that the note I had just received was an endorsement too of the previous few years.

It wasn't only the last two weeks that had given me the confidence to speak out, the belief I had something to say. I had known for some time that I had been changed by my experience of Sudan and that I could never return to the life I had led before coming to this continent. What this letter said to me was that the lives that had changed my own were also of interest to others.

A few days later, I had another audience at the Nigerian embassy. The gentleman I met had the authority this time to grant me a visa, but only if he decided I had a valid case. He seemed more sympathetic than the frosty official I had first encountered. As I related my reasons for wanting to visit his country, he nodded his head and scribbled in a notebook he held in front of him. When I described my ordeals in Chad, the hardships and difficulties I had endured, he seemed sympathetic. The fact that my sister was teaching in Nigeria also seemed to count in my favour.

'It's highly irregular, Mr. McIvor,' he said when I had finished. 'We normally don't provide visas for our country unless you live in the place where you are requesting one. But I think it would be wrong of us to send you back to Sudan without visiting your sister. You'll have a visa tomorrow.'

After thanking him profusely I rose to leave, but he had a final question he wanted to ask. 'Will you be coming back this way to Sudan? Surely it would be better to fly than to go through that ordeal again.'

Since arriving in N'djamena I had addressed that question to myself many times. What will you do? Will you come back this way? The prospect of another journey like the one I had just completed seemed daunting and scary whenever I thought about it. I was sure too that my sister would lend me the money for the flight I needed, if I asked her. An alternative was possible, but the voice that had urged me to continue when I thought of giving up had not disappeared. It was still there urging me to come back this way again, telling me I would find a similarly protective group of people to look after me on the return journey. Didn't I have my letters too, and proof that they would help me when I was in trouble?

Most of all, the request from the Irish Times was like a new challenge, pointing another direction to my life in Africa. It would be foolish to decline such an opportunity without finding out where it might take me.

'Yes,' I replied. 'I will come this way again.'

'But why?' he asked.

'Because there is something I have still to do. There is business here I have not yet completed.'

Afterword – The Road Ahead

A few days later I arrived in Kano, northern Nigeria. My sister had never believed I would make the journey. I spent the next few days in bed recovering from a nasty attack of dysentery.

'I think you should fly back to Sudan,' was her constant refrain throughout the several weeks I spent with her, but I was determined to return to El Geneina the same way I had come.

Othman's contacts proved reliable. From N'Djamena I found another convoy heading east and spent a further week retracing my previous route. The food we were carrying seemed desperately needed in the villages we passed through, but ended up instead in the warehouses of Abeché.

Khalid had not yet returned from the fighting in the north of the country. I was a guest in his house for several days before his brother found me a lift back to El Geneina. I departed in the early morning. When I asked the driver several hours later where we were, he told me we were in Sudan. There was no fence, checkpoint, soldiers, signpost or natural feature to indicate we had crossed into a different country.

'You have lost weight,' Mohammed said when he saw me. 'But at least you are alive.'

The next day we visited all the people whose letters had helped me. 'Didn't I tell you the Sheikh has no enemies,' his deputy said when I told him how influential his leader had been.

Several weeks later I was back in Dublin. I wrote several stories for the Irish Times about the conflict in Chad, the diversion of food aid and the increasing conflict between nomads and settled peoples that were taking place across the Sahara.

I was also asked to give some lectures on my experience as a teacher in Sudan to aid workers from Ireland planning to go overseas, but I was not yet finished with my own travels. Some months later I was offered a teaching job in southern Algeria, and found myself back again on the continent that continued to fascinate and intrigue me. I wrote another series of articles for the Irish Times on what I observed during a series of trans-desert journeys.

During one of my trips to Niger, we came across a number of vehicles being driven by French tourists. They were taking second hand cars across the Sahara to resell in West Africa. We had to rescue them from the desert where they had broken down.

'Do you think that the Sahara is like one of your beaches back home?' the driver of the truck I was in asked them. 'The principal thing we have learned after centuries of living here is to respect this environment. You would do better to learn that too'

Some time after leaving Sudan I discontinued my Muslim practice. However I have retained a deep respect for the religion I witnessed in North Africa and the form in which it was manifested by many of the people I encountered during my travels. The stereotype of an intolerant and fanatical Islam predominates in the West, but the Sufis I met and the followers of Mahmud Taha manifested none of these char-acteristics. Many people are prepared to accept the argument that Christianity should not be judged by its more intolerant episodes and individuals, that its true meaning is something different. I believe this same latitude should be extended to other religions.

I decided to give up teaching when I completed my contract in Algeria. My interest in development issues and my desire to understand more about the lives of the people in Africa who had influenced me, pushed me into the aid world which I have been a part of ever since. That work has taken me to Morocco, Zimbabwe and Mozambique as well as the islands of the Caribbean.

I have never quite abandoned some of the reservations I had

from my time in Sudan and Chad about the value of aid in general. Charity, development work, helping others is a noble cause but needs to be tempered with a constant questioning of what we are doing. It also needs to be accompanied by humility. Failing to acknowledge that the lives of the people we assist are every bit as complex and valuable as our own makes us poor aid workers. The people we help will also begin to manifest the qualities of dependency and passivity we so often lament.

'Treat us like fools and we will behave like fools,' is a remark I heard from a farmer in Mozambique, complaining about the way he was treated by an aid agency during a recent emergency.

I have not returned to Sudan since I left it, a country I owe so much to in terms of what it taught me, but like many of the teachers who worked there during that period I have continued to follow its fortunes (or misfortunes) from a distance.

Most of its subsequent history has caused shock and horror rather than any sense that this is a country moving forward. Since 1983 when Nimeiri introduced Sharia law and prompted another war between the north and south it has lurched from one crisis to the next.

Although some tensions in Darfur were present when I was there, there was little evidence to indicate the explosion that would later happen. People in Sudan used to joke about the country next door. 'What a terrible place to live,' they would say about Chad. 'How lucky we are to be here, but now a considerable part of the population of western Darfur is exiled in the very country they used to ridicule.

There are also many more refugee camps in El Geneina than were present when I was there. These are no longer for external refugees but for the displaced population of the province. Thousands of Darfurians have fled persecution, torture, plunder and pillage from the Government and its armed militias who have turned the area into a war zone and El Geneina into one of the worst places to live on earth.

I find it difficult to relate my memories of the friendliness of Sudan's people, the generosity, openness and curiosity I found in the 1980s to what has subsequently happened to that country. In particular the spirit of tolerance I encountered among the Sufi orders and the people who were influential in my own conversion is difficult to reconcile with the religious intolerance and bigotry that Sudan is now known for.

Whenever the thought of what has happened there becomes too depressing to contemplate, I remember the individuals and personalities I interacted with. I think of the warmth and hospitality shown to a complete stranger arriving in their communities, the citizen of a former colonial power with a not very benign history of involvement in their country. Wouldn't it have been more reasonable to expect the opposite of what in fact greeted me?

Such characteristics among a people can never be eliminated completely. While corruption, greed, political ambitions and prejudice among political and religious leaders can begin to colour an entire society, I choose to believe that the more innate characteristics of the Sudanese people will eventually shine through.

Further Reading

Moorehead Alan, *The Blue Nile*, Penguin 1962. (A history of the Nile in the 19th century)

Moorehead Alan, *The White Nile*, Penguin 1962. (A follow up to the first book.)

Salih, Tayeb, *The Season of Migration to the North*, Heinemann, 1969 (Stories by a Sudanese author of life along the Nile in northern Sudan)

De Waal, Alex, *Famine that Kills: Darfur, Sudan, 1984 – 1985*, Oxford University Press, 1989

Flint, Julie and De Waal, Alex, Darfur: *A New History of a Long War*, Zed Books, 2008

Useful Web Sites

www.savethechildren.co.uk – (Save the Children)

www.darfurinfo.org – (Information on the crisis in Darfur)

www.royalafricansociety.org – (organization that promotes greater understating of African issues)

www.reliefweb.int – (good site to keep up with humanitarian developments in Sudan)